On examining Shakespeare's numerous commentators, and other records of the times, it appears that no censure was ever cast, no unfavorable sentiment entertained of the unjust judge, the injurious merchant, the undutiful daughter and prodigal lover. What an idea does this give of the English nation when such sentiments could be applauded!
Cleric Richard Hole, in *Shylock* by John Gross

Antonio and Bassanio are pale shadows compared with this gaunt, tragic figure, whose love of his race is as deep as life; who pleads the cause of a common humanity against the cruelties of prejudice; whose very hatred has in it something of the nobility of patriotic passion; whose heart is stirred with tender memories even in the midst of his lament over the stolen ducats; who, in the end, is dismissed, unprotesting, to insult and oblivion.
Sir Walter Raleigh, in *Shylock* by John Gross

In the modern world, the Jew has perpetually been on trial; still today the Jew is on trial, in the person of the Israeli – and this modern trial of the Jew, this trial which never ends, begins with the trial of Shylock.
Philip Roth, *Operation Shylock*

How came they here?
What burst of Christian hate,
What persecution, merciless and blind,
Drove o'er the sea – that desert desolate –
These Ishmaels and Hagars of mankind?
Henry Wadsworth Longfellow, 'The Jewish Cemetery at Newport'

I have felt sorry that so many Jews…fail to recognize Shylock as their brother, and turn their backs on him. I have never found Shylock to be the villain against whom Jews keep protesting as a libel of their kind. To the contrary, he is one of the few heroic Jews in classic literature, perhaps even the only one.
Ben Hecht, *Shylock, My Brother* [unfinished]
(quoted by Stuart Schoffman in "A Stone for His Slingshot" *The Jewish Review of Books*, Spring 2014.)

The Trials of Shylock:
An Actor's Inquiry

Alan Bergreen

www.hugejam.com
2024

Copyright © 2024 Alan Bergreen

All rights reserved.

First published by Huge Jam
Gravenhurst, England, 2024

ISBN: 978-1-916604-13-1

Every effort has been made to ensure that the information in this book is correct. The author and publisher hereby disclaim any liability to any party for any impact caused by errors or omissions.

NOTE: *The Trials of Shylock: An Actor's Inquiry* should be understood in its specific historical context; that of British Mandatory Palestine and the struggle of the Jewish people and survivors of the Holocaust for haven in the land promised them by Britain under the Balfour Declaration and the League of Nations mandate. No other conflict or context is implied.

Front cover image: Maurycy Gottlieb, *Portrait of a Jew*
Back cover image: The Jewish Brigade Group, British Army 1944
Images that are not public domain are used under licence and credited in captions.
Chapter decoration is taken from the first folio edition of 'The Merchant of Venice' 1623.

DEDICATION

To the Memory of My Parents
Sholem and Miriam Bergreen
who instilled in me a love of Justice and of Zion.

And to my loving sister, **Marsha Bergreen**,
an extraordinary teacher of gifted and talented children.

* * *

To two great men of the American and French theatres, teachers and mentors:

Sanford Meisner of the *Group Theatre*, and *The Neighborhood Playhouse*
in New York.

Guy Romans, Homme de théâtre, Directeur de *L'Ecole du Vieux Colombier*,
who introduced me to the legacy of Jacques Copeau, Louis Jouvet,
Charles Dullin, and a vision of what theatre could be.

* * *

In gravest sorrow for Zion's tears; past and present.
7th October 2023

"A wonderful example of the kind of research actors (and directors as well) need to do in figuring out how plays best speak to ourselves and our audiences. This is a prodigious work with awesome scope."

Professor Sharon Marie Carnicke

https://sharoncarnicke.com

Founder of *The Stanislavsky Institute for the 21st Century*
Author of *'Dynamic Acting through Active Analysis'*, *'Checking Out Chekhov'* and *'Stanislavsy in Focus'*.

SPECIAL THANKS:

To those who took early interest in my work and offered valuable encouragement and assistance to my efforts:

Sharon Marie Carnicke,
Professor, Dramatic Arts and Slavic Languages and Literatures
University of Southern California, School of Dramatic Arts.

Miriam Bailin, Professor Emerita, Department of English,
Washington University in St. Louis.

Fabienne Romans, my good friend.

I should also like to thank my editor, Jacqueline Tobin, for bringing this project to fruition.

—AB.

'the worst passions of human nature are nurtured by undeserved persecution'

—Henry Irving, 1879
pictured here in his role as Shylock.

CONTENTS

Foreword 1
   The Problem 2
Disclaimer 5
PART ONE 7
The Question: Is 'The Merchant of Venice' an Antisemitic Play? 9
   Antisemitism: A Litmus Test 12
   My Son the Moneylender 14
   "The Green-Eyed Monster" and Its Victims 14
   Antisemitism: Shakespeare's or Our Own? 16
   From Insult to Injury: *Stereotype, Racism, & Demonology* 18
My Shylock Project: *God of Vengeance vs. God of Love* 21
Manifesto 24
Actor's Notebook 28
   Irony 33
   The Revengers: Murder Most Foul or Poetic Justice? 36
   The Heart of the Problem 39
   "Hath Not a Jew Eyes", Indeed! 41
   The Jewish Question and the Lure of Anachronism 42
   Shylock and Antonio 44
   Antonio and Bassanio 46
   Shylock and Portia 48

Portia's Realm: Belmont as Bloomsbury 49
Shylock and Blood Libel: The Unkindest Cut of All? 51
"The Hated Rival" 55
Stereotypes and Consequences 60
Villain, Martyr, or Everyman? 62
Actor's Memoir: *Recollections Profound and Profane* 63
"Now that's a *real* antisemite!" 63
Conversations with Morris Carnovsky 64
"Out of the mouths of WASPS" 66
A Mixed (Up) Marriage 67
Revelations of a "Union Maid" 68
A Drama School Faux Pas 69
When the Quality of Mercy is Strained, Indeed! 71
What Comes by Chance - A Shylock Found 72
Stranger in a Strange Land 73
Concept and Setting
The Mandate Connection: *A Political Odyssey* 76
PART TWO **83**
Adaptation and Treatment **93**
Afterword: *Journey's End for Now* 250
APPENDIX: *Scenescapes* 253
Notes 274
Bibliography 278
Index 281
About the Author 290

FOREWORD

The *Merchant of Venice (MV)* has long been a troubling enigma to me. First, because of the seemingly bigoted portrait it presents of its signature character, "the Jew, Shylock". Second, because of my personal inability to reconcile such sentiments with Shakespeare himself, a man and writer of extraordinary sensibilities and stature in the world of letters and the theatre; a realm I sought to inhabit as an actor. This sense of cognitive dissonance, and the nagging distaste that resulted from it, inclined me to avoid the play altogether for a long period despite a keen desire to engage with a variety of other Shakespeare plays and characters.

My perspective began to change, however, because of the influence of a great voice and Shakespeare teacher with whom I trained, Kristin Linklater, whose techniques for "freeing the natural voice" and "freeing Shakespeare's voice" opened to me an emotional palette and insights that transformed my view of Shylock and revealed possibilities for interpretation of a wholly different character than the hateful ones of old.

I remember in particular Kristin's description of Shylock as "a man driven to the end of his tether"; a seemingly simple characterisation but one that had particular resonance for me at the time and opened a flood of previously untapped emotions. The results of this emotional recall powerfully released through her vocal techniques, produced a portrayal of Shylock at once vulnerable and enraged, balefully brimming with tears of pain and anger, undiminished by stale ethnic stereotype. I think that even she was surprised at the results!

This experience revealed to me the possibility of a fully human Shylock possessed of injured humanity rather than inveterate evil. Thus I embarked upon a probing inquiry, as a detective might (and as an actor should), into what *MV* really was in Shakespeare's eyes. What his motives might have been in creating it. What the guilt of Shylock truly is in the circumstances of the play. And what guilt, if any, Shakespeare bears in the promotion of antisemitism in the larger culture, historically. As an investigator admittedly sympathetic to the "defendant", I also wished to explore the possibility of "extenuating circumstances"; what *MV* could be today if divorced from the antisemitic canards long associated with the play and embodied most incriminatingly in Shakespeare's provocative creation, Shylock.

What follows is the product of that search.

* * *

The Problem

MV presents modern actors and directors with two complex challenges.

First: how to understand and then portray the signature character, Shylock – a man in the throes of such seemingly irrational hatred towards Antonio, the merchant of Venice, that he resorts to homicidal mutilation as a weapon against him.

Second: how to present this sadistic excess so that a modern audience does not view Shylock's Jewish ethnicity as the intrinsic source of his perversity – a hazard long associated with the play.

In an exploration of *MV* based upon historical research, personal memoir, and long-term residence in the state of Israel, I have sought to reconsider long-held assumptions regarding the parties to this drama in the hope of altering perception of the play's meaning.

My approach is that of an actor seeking a character for performance rather than a critic focused on dramatic tradition or original intent.

I admit at the outset to an ulterior motive: I seek to turn *MV*'s antisemitism on its head by exposing the cruelty of Shylock's tormentors and the impact of degradation upon his conduct; to transform a derisive comedy at the expense of "the Jew" into a psychological study of a broken man at the end of his tether. And to render the play a critique of antisemitism rather than a vehicle for it.

In addition, through a proposed treatment in narrative form, envisioning how my concept might be realised in performance, (Part 2), I hope to reframe Shylock's image and *MV*'s meaning through characterisation and setting without violence to the spoken text. Thereby levelling powerful rebuke at promoters of intolerance who exist behind a façade of high "Christian" principles and elite social status.

The very fact that *MV* is listed as a classical comedy in Shakespeare's canon (meaning it ends happily) is a forewarning of the offences this book examines; for its "happy ending" revolves around the breaking of an innocent man, driven to extremes by adversity and abuse, the destruction of his business and family, and his forced conversion to Christianity – an outcome that can hardly be viewed as "happy" by a modern audience with any sense of justice and tolerance for cultural and religious diversity.

Furthermore, I argue that *MV* says more about London's historical attitudes towards Jews than those of Venice; an assumption useful for a modern context. Thus, a setting is proposed to illuminate that relationship in stark Jewish-British polarities: British Mandatory

Palestine in the years 1945-48, a period fraught with existential conflict pitting Imperial Britain against the Jews.

This choice offers striking similarities to Shakespeare's Venetian characters, with British colonial authorities – a class often contemptuous of Jews – in parallel with their bigoted Venetian counterparts. In the case of Britain, denial of Jewish refuge in Palestine during the Nazi genocide compounded this contempt, resulting in criminal complicity in the enormity of the Holocaust. These policies evoked immense outrage in many quarters, within Britain and without, leading to the violent overthrow of British colonial rule in Palestine by Jews who, taking a leaf from Shylock's book, demonstrated to their overlords that: *"The villainy you teach me I will execute. And ... I will better the instruction!"*

The magnitude of Shylock's rage and mania can then be understood in the context of national trauma and in the wake of genocide, adding a moving dimension of injured humanity to the character, eschewing the bigoted view of Shylock – traditionally held – as the embodiment of inveterate Jewish evil. In this context, Shylock's violence can be seen in modern terms of psychology, social dynamics, and political struggle, rather than medieval stereotypes and blood libels.

In place of demonic images of old rooted in a long history of canards directed against the Jews, I propose a modern vehicle for reflection on intolerance and its consequences, exposing the religious and racial bigotry, class prejudice, and antisemitism at the heart of our civilisation that continue to afflict its victims.

Uncovering Shylock's humanity, however flawed, isn't the only theme my treatment lays bare. It draws attention to the ancillary theme of extremes: the limits to which the oppressed may go in retribution for the abuses they have suffered. An unresolved moral dilemma that has much to say, dramatically, about the state of our world today.

DISCLAIMER

What follows is a polemic. A polemic rooted in historical argument and memoir, leading to a dramatic political setting of *MV*.

I wish at the outset to avoid the possibility of misunderstanding, or of injustice to British and Christian readers in what follows. Because I am casting Shakespeare's antisemitic Venetians as British establishment figures in Mandatory Palestine, my treatment of the play will, inevitably, focus heavily upon the vices of that social elite, its antisemitism, and the abuses of British policy towards Europe's Jews seeking refuge in Palestine – all elements which, sadly, did exist and are well-documented.

I feel safe in saying that many of my British friends, Jewish and non-Jewish alike, would likely agree with much of this criticism within a proper context, acknowledging the existence of anti-reactionary forces within British society as well. Unfortunately, the focus here, dictated by the given circumstances of the play, does not allow for quite the diversity of views that I would prefer. I wish to make it clear that, for my part, this in no way reflects a desire to be prejudicial or vindictive towards the British people as a whole. But Shakespeare offers no sympathetic alternatives to the figures of Antonio, Gratiano, et al. vis-à-vis things Jewish, and that is the foundation from which I must work if I wish to remain within the parameters of the play as written.

While I feel that criticism of reactionary elements within the British establishment who sought to subvert the policies of Liberal Britain is warranted, I recognise that antipathy towards Jews was not shared by all. There were a variety of philosemitic influences in British history, ranging from the liberal evangelical Christian Zionists of the 19th century (including the famed abolitionist, William Wilberforce), to the Manchester Circle (Lloyd George, Arthur Balfour, Winston Churchill, Chaim Weizmann) which conceived the Balfour Declaration, to the maverick military figures of Orde Wingate, "father" of the Haganah Jewish defence force in Palestine and Lt.-Col. Henry J. Patterson, commander of the Jewish Legion during WWI that saw distinguished service at Gallipoli and the Palestine campaign. There were also the socialists of the democratic left, such as the great Labour leaders Aneurin Bevan, Richard Crossman, and Michael Foot, as well as the future Prime Minister, Harold Wilson, among others, who were outspoken, progressive friends of the Jewish People and Zionism.[1] I would have been delighted if *MV* had provided an outlet for such sentiments, but, alas, Elizabethan England and Shakespeare were not so inclined, and European culture at the time demonstrated no particular spirit of ecumenism towards the Jews. I find this regrettable, but my objective here is to reinterpret *MV*, not rewrite it. I must therefore work with the material as I find it.

I should like to make it clear that my interpretation seeks to expose and indict the actions of a certain political class, not condemn an entire nation. I do not wish to generalise indiscriminately or unjustly, nor do I hold all Britons or all Christians responsible for the abuses of the past. I fully reject judgments based upon collective guilt and religious or national association. But I do believe it important to understand the past while not "visiting the iniquities of the fathers upon the sons". I hope that my efforts will be understood and accepted in that spirit.

—*A.B. August 2023*

PART ONE

Maurycy Gottlieb, *Shylock and Jessica*

THE QUESTION:

Is 'The Merchant of Venice' an Antisemitic Play?

"One would have to be blind, deaf and dumb not to recognise that Shakespeare's grand, equivocal comedy *The Merchant of Venice* is nevertheless a profoundly anti-semitic work."
– *Harold Bloom[2]*

"It has often occurred to me that as beautiful as that speech is ('Hath not a Jew eyes?') it could also have been made by a hyena or baboon. All he's saying is: Don't we breathe? But that's not the way you judge people, and that's not the way Shakespeare judged people either."
– *Robert Brustein[3]*

"Shylock is the English archetype of the villainous Jew. Those who talk about how humanistic, universal, and empathetic his portrait is, are ignoring not only how it was perceived at the time but its historical consequences."
– *Robert Wistrich[4]*

The controversy surrounding *MV*'s putative antisemitism and its possible complicity in the scheme of historic oppression is heightened by uncertainty regarding Shakespeare's true intent. And the painful knowledge of where this abuse has led has inclined many directors, pre- and, especially, post-WWII, to drastically alter the traditional staging of the work. Some of high repute have even argued against reviving the play altogether.[5]

I am neither neutral nor indifferent on these matters. I don't assume reflexively that Shakespeare couldn't possibly have been an antisemite, neither would I turn a blind eye to such a flaw or view it benignly in deference to his genius. Nor do I reflexively assume the worst. How *MV* is understood and interpreted is ultimately a complex question, given contradictory possibilities.

To approach a conclusion regarding Shakespeare's intent, we must first ask a number of questions:

- Is Shylock, "the Jew", ever referred to in other than pejorative terms, or is any other Jewish figure of noble stature arrayed against him, referred to in the abstract, or so represented in any other Shakespeare play?
- Is there an instance in literature or the idiom of any language in which comparison to Shylock carries other than pejorative connotations? Would we refer to Einstein as "the great Shylock of science", Horowitz, as "the Shylock of the classical keyboard", or Bellow and Singer, as "the Nobel Shylocks of literature"?
- If *MV* is not antisemitic, as many wish to believe, why has it been "mistakenly" construed that way with such regularity? And why have major efforts to reinterpret the piece and soften or eliminate its antisemitic overtones required elaborate effort and caused considerable controversy among the public, critics, actors, and directors alike? And most devastatingly: why was *MV* a favourite of Nazi producers and audiences?[6]

Let's ask another audacious question. If Shylock were not a Jew, would *MV* be more than Elizabethan *Grand Guignol?* Other literary virtues notwithstanding, is it not Shylock's status as a Jew and the multiplicity of "Jewish Questions" ranging from the Biblical to the contemporary that arise from that status, that fuel with such intensity our concern for the character (either pro or con) and has compelled interest in the play over centuries? Would, "hath not a (Turk) eyes" – though equally true in principle – have had the same resonance in the cultural consciousness of the West?

Shylock, as a character, is not, in fact, very Jewish, or not very fully or accurately developed in that sense. In the words of John Gross in his illuminating work, *Shylock: A Legend and its Legacy*: "Shylock's stage-Judaism is a pseudo-religion, a fabrication: there is no true piety in it, and nothing to hold him back as he pursues his revenge".[7] Yet, is it not his iconic status as a "Jew", however imperfectly portrayed, that is the burning source of engagement and conflict in the play which cannot be ignored? This leads to the question: what is it about the "Jew", as a concept, that leads to feelings as intense, diverse, and obsessive as fear, love, or loathing in the gentile mind?

Whether Shakespeare was consciously aware of the potential inherent in *MV* to subvert the prevailing prejudices of his day, and whether he set out to do so, based on available evidence, is highly unlikely. There is no indication that "social reform" was on his mind. If he had wanted to do so there might have been avenues open to him. Writing on Biblical themes (as Racine chose to do) with depictions of Jewish warriors and kings would not have been out of the question and might even have been popular at the box office. But this was not his wont, and it is idle to speculate on historical, "what-ifs".

It is only because of the progressive breakdown of traditional Christian thinking through the impact of the "Enlightenment", advancing secularism (and perhaps a little humanising "Judaisation" of our culture, as well) that assumptions long held in Christian society regarding Shylock's inherent evil have been called into question. At the same time, I think the argument is true that Shakespeare, in the expanse of his humanity and genius, gives us in the character of Shylock a complex human being with the potential to be understood in a different light, if we have the inclination to do so. A challenge I embrace.

Antisemitism: A Litmus Test

How does our interpretation of Shylock and his relationship with his tormentors reflect our own preconceptions of Jews and our own assumptions regarding their moral, personal, and social status vis-à-vis the Christian world? These questions were brought into focus for me while watching an interchange between Sir John Barton of the RSC and two prominent company members, David Suchet and Patrick Stewart, who had both played the role. Barton emphasised that *MV* was a play about a "bad Jew" beset by "bad Christians", while David Suchet agonised over how Shylock could have fallen to such debasement as to seek revenge.

Stewart, by contrast, was innovative in declaring he wasn't overly concerned with Shylock's "Jewishness" at all, but rather on what, in Stanislavsky's parlance, might be called his "action" (and, I may say, this was put to very good effect in his rendering of Act 3, scene 1 from which one came away with the feeling that Shylock's remorse at the loss of his diamonds was actually his devastation at the loss of his child). But it was the apparent consternation at the prospect of a Jew seeking revenge that "prostrated me" (to paraphrase GBS), and, to my mind, opened a remarkable can of (conceptual) worms.

When a Danish prince seeks revenge, declaring it outright – *"O vengeance!"* – against a murderous, usurping uncle, we don't object.

When a new-crowned English king seeks revenge against an entire nation that he is led to believe has usurped his royal prerogatives and territories, we give him license to wreak devastation on the heads of innocent multitudes (way more than a "pound of flesh") and we dub him a "hero".

When a Moor takes revenge on an innocent and defenceless wife, we find it titillating (or at least we don't hold it against Moors in general).

When a deformed tyrant takes revenge on just about everyone around him (largely, as he himself admits, because he can't get laid) we are delighted with his ghoulishness.

But a Jew? A Jew seeking revenge – and against a Christian, no less? Albeit a Christian who has publicly abused and humiliated him, defiled his person and the symbols of his ethnicity, broken his trade and his family… We can't have that! It strikes at the very order of things in the traditional Christian universe! A universe where far lesser offences result in vengeful duels, murderous retribution, and vindictive bloodletting with regularity!

Therein, I submit, lies the crux of the play and its significance. How *MV* is interpreted, and its characters construed and balanced, is a virtual litmus test of antisemitism, even detecting trace elements of the toxin camouflaged behind the most liberal façade.

I would argue that Shylock, in the given circumstances of the play, is not inherently a "bad" Jew or a "bad" anything else for that matter. He is by all indications an avid businessman, a strict but caring father, a law-abiding resident of Venice, and a civil member of society.

For his pains, he is derided, spat upon, harassed, and publicly humiliated by a succession of "goyishe" ne'er-do-wells who take it as axiomatic that their superior status allows them the liberty of using and abusing "the Jew" with impunity. One can only imagine the liberties that would be extended to a Christian similarly wronged to avenge his honour, or the indulgence extended to him if, in extremis, his passions got the better of him.

My Son the Moneylender

There is a particularly pernicious history of contempt coupled with envy towards Jews in European society because of their prominence in trade and finance; a position which has often put them at odds with both upper and lower classes.

While anti-Jewish prejudice has been pervasive – especially among the upper classes in Britain and in a tradition of British literature – in modern times the British have avoided the large-scale violence against Jews seen in Russia, Eastern Europe and ultimately Germany, thereby justifying in their minds an image of civility and tolerance. Passive aggression, however, can have deadly consequences, as I shall later discuss. For the moment, let us simply consider the possibility that *MV* and the provocations Shylock experiences say more about the prejudices of London than of Venice.

"The Green-Eyed Monster" and Its Victims

Iago's admonition to Othello (3.3), suggesting Desdemona's infidelity, unleashes a force of jealousy that drives the general to murderous extremes. So too, the effects of 'the green-eyed monster' can be felt on social and economic levels with demonstratively ill-effects. Regarding the Jews, a pernicious history of contempt and envy has been seen repeatedly in European society because of their prominence in trade and finance – a position often viewed with hostility by both upper and lower classes.

The fact that Jewish pre-eminence in this sphere is largely the product of Christian prejudice and discrimination – i.e., generations of exclusion from land ownership, guilds and other sources of Christian livelihood and social diversification – has mattered little in the uncharitable assessment of the Jew as usurer and worshipper of money (a charge often levelled by devout Christian and devout Marxist alike).

Moreover, the debt of Europe's economies to these distasteful "Jewish pursuits", and the willingness of Pope, Emperor, and Prime Minister to exploit Jewish commercial prowess even as they disparaged it, seems to elicit no embarrassment. The British have been particularly passive-aggressive in this regard, denigrating Jews in a variety of ways and under a variety of ideological and social guises for the "sins" of economic initiative and social mobility; the very qualities their sclerotic class system has often lacked (they also resent Americans for much the same reasons).

Indeed, passive aggression and outright bigotry have taken their toll, even extending to the treatment of eminent figures of Jewish descent in public life such as Benjamin Disraeli. In his exhaustive study of British antisemitism, *Trials of the Diaspora: A History of Anti-Semitism in England,* (Oxford University Press), Anthony Julius describes the shocking calumnies directed against this most eminent of British Prime Ministers:

> In the manner of anti-Semitic discourse, the abuse was both inventive and stale. Disraeli was a "lump of dirt," a "Fagin." He was "Judas," "Jewish Dizzy," the "Jewish Chief," "Sir Benjamin de Judah," and "Chief Rabbi Benjamin." He was "a very Hebrew of Hebrews," the "Jew Earl, Philo-Turkish Jew and Jew Premier" and the "traitorous Jew," the "haughty Jew," and the "abominable" … a "man of the East," an "Asiatic." … (H)e was represented as Shylock ("our modern Shylock"); many related him to the Devil ("the most authentic incarnation of the Evil One") … ritually murdering the infant Britannia … (with) Gladstone … the distressed

mother, arriving perhaps too late to save her child. And there was a note sounded for the first time, but to be repeated many times thereafter: the Jews want war, against the national interest.

Moreover, Julius cites Chaucer, Shakespeare, Dickens, Thomas Carlyle, William Cobbett, W.E. Gladstone, Bertrand Russell, Queen Victoria, Ernest Bevin, and George Orwell, as among the prominent literary and political figures past and modern whose uncomplimentary views towards Jews were hardly veiled.

With such calumnies well-accepted in the minds of many of the British ruling classes and society at large, is it any wonder that passive aggression might one day have deadly consequences in a time of existential crisis?

Antisemitism: Shakespeare's or Our Own?

When it comes to "the Jew" in Christian eyes, both in *MV* and in the larger Christian world for many centuries, doing business has been tantamount to "money-grubbing" replete with a variety of derisive stereotypes to reinforce the point – a pervasive prejudice that lives on subliminally and even overtly in the minds of audiences to this day.

So much of what is interpreted as objectionable about Shylock is projected upon him by the bigotry of the Christians in the play or reflected in the prejudices and preconceptions of audiences a bit too eager to align themselves with "superior" aristocratic sensibilities – in some circles even to the point of high-culture antisemitism. But when the same functions are performed by wealthier Christians, they enjoy the status of "high finance", "provision of credit", "profit margins", etc. (not to mention John Houseman and Smith Barney! *"They make money the old-fashioned way…they earn it!"*).

Are such pejoratives in the play itself?

Can there be justification for these assumptions?

Well, in fact, Shylock earns his money the "old fashioned way" too! And it is interesting to note that Shakespeare makes no mention of him doing so underhandedly or by means of excessive rates or devious practices. Shylock's only "crime", as it were in the eyes of the church and society of his day, is the fact that he is a moneylender and that to be blunt about it he's "doing business while Jewish". Nothing more. The fact that he's preoccupied with business is altogether natural and no different from the preoccupations of Christian businessmen and merchants, including his nemesis, Antonio.

When Shylock enters the play, he is heard mulling over the sum of 3,000 ducats which is taken by some to indicate his total obsession with money. But in fact, his engrossment is not a matter of devotion or obsession, but rather a matter of business clearly indicated by the action of the scene – he is considering a proposition for a loan requested by Bassanio on behalf of Antonio. What else would a businessman be doing under the circumstances? It is interesting to note in this regard that Antonio's melancholy at the play's opening is attributed by his friends to his anxiety about his cargoes at sea and the potential profits or losses they represent, yet Antonio isn't dubbed a "money grubber" for all that. Evidently, "what's gravy for the Christian merchant (goose), isn't gravy for the Jewish moneylender (gander)".[8]

These attitudes reveal a distasteful undercurrent of prejudice and condescension based on stereotypes of "the avaricious Jew" that linger even in the minds of modern audiences who, despite living in an age of full blown capitalism upon which much of benefit in their lives depends, still view Shylock and his business activities as debased and beneath them. As if theatregoers are all aristocrats! The next time they need a loan it will be interesting to see if they confront their bankers with the term "money grubber"![9]

From Insult to Injury: *Stereotype, Racism, & Demonology*

Shakespeare says little about Shylock in the given circumstances of *MV* by way of description or action that is intrinsically pejorative in modern terms, or that couldn't have been said about him, himself, in his later professions of businessman and moneylender – a trade in which both he and his father engaged. Which makes it the more questionable that such views can be imputed to the text itself. What is more, the grotesque depictions of Shylock with a bright red wig, redolent of the devil, and crudely hooked nose, a staple of antisemitic racism which became ubiquitous for centuries are nowhere found in Shakespeare's text. They appear to be bigoted accretions of subsequent generations which became theatrical conventions, as the following interchange between two distinguished Shakespeare scholars in the *New York Review of Books* (October 14, 2010), suggests:

> In response to:
> Shakespeare & Shylock from the September 30, 2010 issue.
> *To the Editors:*
>
> In an otherwise illuminating review of the Public Theater's production of *The Merchant of Venice* [*NYR*, September 30], Stephen Greenblatt writes that in "the earliest productions, Shylock was played with a bright red wig and a grotesque hooked nose." There's no evidence for this in Shakespeare's play at all—in contrast to Christopher Marlowe's caricature Barabas in *The Jew of Malta*, who does resemble this medieval stereotype. The tradition that Shakespeare's Shylock was "a red-hair'd Jew" derives from a forgery perpetrated by the nineteenth-century scholar John Payne Collier, but not even Collier says anything about a grotesque or hooked nose. Other than the loose upper garment that he wears (which Shylock calls "my Jewish gaberdine"), there's nothing in *The Merchant of Venice* that visibly distinguishes Shylock from his Christian adversaries. And that's exactly Shakespeare's point.
>
> James Shapiro
> Columbia University
> New York City

Stephen Greenblatt replies:

I am grateful for James Shapiro's welcome reminder that, for all we know, Richard Burbage—if he was, as is sometimes thought, the first Shylock—may not have looked significantly different from Antonio: after all, that is, as I remarked in my article, a possible implication of Portia's question (cut by Daniel Sullivan), "Which is the merchant here and which the Jew?" But for my description of the old theatrical tradition of playing Shylock with red wig and hooked nose, I was relying on the earliest surviving allusion: not Collier's nineteenth-century forged elegy to Burbage but rather a much earlier source, one whose authenticity has not, as far I know, been called into question. In 1664, Thomas Jordan (circa 1614–1685), who had before the Civil War been an actor with the King's Revels Company, wrote a ballad retelling the plot of Shakespeare's play. The ballad is pedestrian enough, but its description of the "vile Jew" provides a highly probable glimpse of Shylock's early stage appearance:

His beard was red; his face was made
Not much unlike a witches.
His habit was a Jewish gown,
That would defend all weather;
His chin turned up, his nose hung down,
And both ends met together.

This is not, to be sure, proof positive, but it is striking that when in the nineteenth century the great actor Edmund Kean performed the part in Drury Lane, spectators were evidently taken by surprise: "By Jove! Shylock in a black wig!"

So, whence did they come?

MY SHYLOCK PROJECT
God of Vengeance vs. God of Love

The problem of reconciling *MV*'s ostensible antisemitism and my attraction to Shakespeare's work lay uncomfortably as a source of dissonance in my mind for many years – the more so because of the vehemence of my opposition to the former and my deep sympathies for the latter. I therefore embarked, after years of avoidance, upon a project to explore as an actor and future director the character of Shylock and to render him fully human and understandable in modern terms.

My goal was to present the play's antisemitism in a manner designed to indict the bigotry of its perpetrators. I sought to do this by discrediting the religious triumphalism-cum-antisemitism historically suggested by the play without resorting to the romanticised convention of "Shylock-as-Martyr", which came into vogue in the 19th century and continues off and on to the present. Both extremes, I felt, diminished the complexity and humanity of Shylock the man, and the emotional nuance and impact of *MV* the play.

What started as a series of actor's notes drawing on various aspects of my own emotional life, historical understanding, and concern for the issues of antisemitism and bigotry, developed into a broader project of research and memoir – including aspects of almost a decade's residence in Israel. In the process, I became confirmed in the view that *MV* should be staged in a way starkly at odds with traditional practices that, even with the best of intentions, often trade to one degree or another in Jewish stereotypes of a distasteful nature and conceptualise the conflict of the play in supersessionist Christian dichotomies:

- God of vengeance vs. God of love
- World of money vs. world of grace
- World of law vs. world of charity
- World of judgment vs. world of mercy
- World of damnation vs. world of salvation[10]

In other words, the world of the Jew (as antisemites see it) vs. the world of the idealised Christian, symbolised by the fairy tale setting: the world of the Rialto vs. the world of Belmont, with Christian nobility and grace triumphing over what to the Christian mind of the period was seen as a "debased" Jewish materialism. In the words of Frank Kermode (cited in *Shylock* by John Gross), "The Merchant of Venice is 'about' judgment, redemption, and mercy... It begins with usury and corrupt love; it ends with harmony and perfect love."[11] Or to be more precise, the love of money vs. the love of community in Christ (with Christianity triumphant). I would submit, the more these dichotomies are stylised in the trappings of innocence, fairy tale, and fantasy, the more removed from serious scrutiny and the more damnable they become, positing prejudices as "truths" of iconic weight beyond the parameters of rational scrutiny or dispute.

In contrast, I saw the play as a hard-edged indictment of Christian hypocrisy; an exposé of class condescension, intolerance, and bigotry masquerading behind a façade of selfless love, mercy, redemption and other so-called "Christian virtues" – pretensions thoroughly belied by the real behaviour of the play's Christians towards "the Jew". There are great sins at the root of Christian civilisation, with the torment of the Jews chief among them; sins which are amply reflected in *MV* on a variety of levels. Even if we think the West has "evolved" beyond its most benighted prejudices, there is no excuse for historical "cleansing" or glib absolution of our culture's forebears and their crimes. To understand *MV* and grasp the mind of Shylock, we must face the world of Christian bigotry and its effect on its victims without evasions or roseate illusions.

I also came to see *MV* as a revealing commentary on the values of "Perfidious Albion", more than a critique of Venice; presciently foreshadowing the imperialist pretensions of generations yet to come who would construct a Belmont-type world coexisting – to their minds, harmoniously – alongside the squalor and degradation of the peoples they saw fit to dominate. Shylock's violence can then be seen in that light as an extreme but understandable reaction to such exploitation and abuse. I therefore sought to realise, for audiences and readers of this book, Shylock's full humanity as an active agent and resister who is struggling to control his fate in the face of unrelenting and dehumanising hostility and all that implies in terms of vulnerabilities and extremes.

I then sought a modern setting dramatically emphasising the characters' relationships within a British-Jewish paradigm. As mentioned above, post-war Mandatory Palestine 1945-48 offered just the stage upon which Shylock could be portrayed as a fully modern, complex man with his vulnerabilities, contradictions, and failings like all other men. Traits further defined by insufferable adversities; personal, social, and political. A departure from both the one-dimensional antisemitic grotesque of old and its limiting modern opposite: the hapless, ineffectual martyr and object of pity.

I find the Palestine setting particularly resonant because of my extensive interest in its history and time spent in Israel among the real-life players in its ongoing drama. I think it provides a context that is at once dramatic, timely, well-suited to the social relationships of the play as I see them and potentially resonant to a larger audience.[12] It is also well-suited to exploring the limits of human endurance and exposing the "high-minded" hypocrisy of Shylock's tormentors.

Given the unhappy and controversial elements of the play it might be preferable to avoid its staging altogether, as some have suggested.[13] But Shakespeare's status and the compelling quality of what he has written make that unlikely to ever be the solution. Shakespeare cannot be ignored, even when his prejudices cannot be condoned. Consequently, if there is a way to plausibly interpret the work as a critique and repudiation of antisemitic bigotry, thereby saving it from the canker of racist repute[14] and turning future audiences against such abuse, it is, in my view, worth exploring.

By means of this approach, I believe that anyone prepared to keep an open mind until the final curtain will see a play that reveals dramatic and unhappy truths of contemporary importance that all in the post-Holocaust world should be obliged to confront and contemplate, and a dramatically probing inquiry into the question of "means and ends" in response to racial and national oppression.

In that spirit, I proceed.

MANIFESTO

MV is a play of consuming interest because it reflects a dilemma of consuming importance: the endemic and persistent curse of antisemitism in Christian society.

Of all Shakespeare's plays, *MV* has inspired the deepest controversy chiefly surrounding its perceived antisemitism. The relationship of this most pernicious prejudice to the play's interpretation and playwright's intent, and its implications regarding our perceptions of Shakespeare the man and writer, have affected Western thinking for centuries.

For traditional antisemites or their genteel fellow travellers, this presents no problem to begin with. But for modern, "enlightened" readers professing no truck with racial or religious bigotry – and anti-Jewish prejudice has taken both these forms – the question of whether *MV* is an antisemitic play and the degree to which it reflects Shakespeare's own sentiments on the matter is a painful one.

Surely, no modern reader who values Shakespeare as a writer of transcendent importance wants to think of him as a bigot or a man willing to appeal to bigotry in others. Yet, in *MV*, classic stereotypes of the Jew as a miscreant, usurer, and object of universal derision abound.

Consequently, Shakespeare himself looms large as a weighty problem for those who wish to believe his moral stature is equal to his insight. For Shakespeare's understanding of humanity is often matched by his reluctance to judge it. And the detachment with which he observes the world proves unsettling. We want to feel that a mind so profound stands clearly for the good – but he won't oblige us. Instead, we are left uncertain and uneasy about his true feelings towards his characters and their behaviour.

This ambiguity is particularly troubling in the post-Holocaust world following a trauma so intense at the heart of our civilisation as to leave no room for an appreciation, in Keats's words, of a Romantic "Negative Capability, that is, when a man is capable of being in uncertainties, Mysteries, doubts, without any irritable reaching after fact and reason". Keats saw that "Shakespeare possessed so enormously" that very capability and that it distinguished him in the world of letters as "a Man of Achievement".[15]

MV is replete with antisemitic characters and opinions, but we are never quite sure in whose voice they ultimately speak or of their larger purpose. And the "uncertainties, Mysteries, doubts…" in this play prove too "irritable" to bear.

We are left suspended in nagging tension over fundamental questions: is *MV* an antisemitic play, or a play about antisemitism? Is it a play written by an antisemite, or a play critical of antisemites? Is it prescriptive or descriptive? And what do we make of "the Jew", himself: a foul, hate-filled wretch, or a flawed anti-hero driven to distraction? And what do we make of ourselves? How *MV* is interpreted in performance depends critically upon the answers to these questions. But the Bard, irritatingly, isn't telling.

What are we to make of that, and how does it affect our perception of Shylock and what he symbolises?

Shakespeare in *MV* runs true to form in stating nothing directly about his intentions. Might it be that this studied reticence challenges us to understand his works in light of our own times and sensibilities? And if so, is the question of what Shylock is and how he became it not then opened to broad interpretation as though by dramatist's invitation? Perhaps we can never know his motives for certain, but the assumption that we are given leave to explore them is an exciting one from an acting perspective.

I will, therefore, take up the challenge of *MV* by charting my own path as an actor and partisan, my eye on dramatic and moral effect rather than scholarly dispassion. In doing so, I will eschew the Holy Grail of "original intent", so often the obsession of the très cultivé, for how grotesque the notion that Shakespeare's imprimatur should make antisemitism palatable or a mark of "high culture", even if he were so inclined. I also must emphasise that as an actor I will be in search of a character, revealing the inner painful paths of that search.

I intend to interpret *MV* as a vehicle of indictment against the antisemites who inhabit it, and those in the real world who identify with them. I further propose, à la Brecht, that we recognise certain unpalatable truths:

- Reaction to oppression need not be "aesthetic."
- Resisters to oppression need not be handsome and heroic.
- Oppression may come wrapped in the gloss of high-mindedness and refinement.[16]

No effort will be made here to enter genteel "conversation" over Shakespeare's "real feelings" about Jews or to engage in attempts to render Shylock "sympathetic" – in effect, "damning by faint praise". Rather I have opted for polemics, because, as Shylock states, "it is my humour"; and because it reflects my deepest feelings and compulsions; and, importantly from the actor's point of view, because of its dramatic utility so clearly required by the play itself. In this regard, to again quote "the Jew", "I am not bound to please…"

Shylock's polemics have had echoes throughout history: *The villainy you teach me, I will execute*, has been the call to arms of liberation movements, ranging from the IRA to the ANC, from the American Revolution to the Russian Revolution. And the human equation in the query "Hath not a Jew eyes?" has found voice in the pleas of the oppressed.

Finally, I believe in the intellectual and moral imperative of "historical reckonings" and withhold sympathy from those inclined to "let bygones be bygones" without understanding what has gone before. The use made of *MV* today must perforce be considered in the light of anti-Jewish persecution historically, a concern not to be blithely dismissed as a preoccupation of the overly sensitive or the parochial. As an actor, I don't wish to be other than partisan in this regard and feel that I honour Shakespeare most on his own terms by being so, for he seems always to prefer lively controversy to deadly orthodoxy – a choice indispensable to the life of the stage.

ACTOR'S NOTEBOOK

"We are such stuff as dreams are made on…"
(Prospero) The Tempest 4.1

I started the process of exploring the mind of Shylock impulsively, half-consciously jotting down a series of actor's notes that drew upon thoughts, experiences and obsessions that had been brewing for years on the subject of *MV* and the culture of antisemitism.

I proceeded in a rather "Rorschach-like" way initially, noting without premeditation or rigid structure a range of free associations and emotions based upon historical research, personal experience, visual imagery, music, and art related to the Jewish experience and history of persecution. I embraced these feelings without inhibition through fantasy and daydream rather than intellectual analysis; a process that even came to invade the vulnerable state between sleep and wake (*"the hour of the wolf"* in the words of Ingmar Bergman[17]) where subconscious impulses and the strength of unfettered emotions are most intense. A state of consciousness which Shakespeare suggests continues with us even into death!

In the immortal lines of Hamlet 3.1:

For in that sleep of death what dreams may come
When we have shuffled off this mortal coil,
Must give us pause …

Hamlet alludes to a level of consciousness beyond the waking life while Prospero, in the quotation from *The Tempest* on the preceding page, places it at the source of our very being, a consciousness of the greatest intensity and even terror.

I feel that the ability to enter this realm and employ the non-conscious or subconscious state through daydream, breathing exercises, meditation, or sleep itself is an invaluable tool in the actor's arsenal and worth honing.

Had I not had the excuse of being an actor, my behaviour might well have been diagnosed as an obsessive-compulsive disorder! A useful "disorder", however, that allowed me to begin to "live" the emotional life of a beleaguered Shylock in preparation for the more structured demands of the text that would follow.

I was more concerned at this stage with emotional freedom and discovery than with potentially inhibiting questions of critical "balance" or aesthetic "nuance". *Shylock, I thought, is not, after all, a "balanced" personality*, and I was not operating as a literary critic or historian, nor was I yet concerned with a refined interpretation of the part. This was a quest for emotional "diamonds in the rough", not polished stones, and it seemed to me that no interpreter of *MV* could do Shylock justice or serve the acting process by being more "dispassionate" in emotional discovery than the character of Shylock is in the life of the play.

All drama – especially as raw as *MV* – is defined by conflict, and the actor approaching Shylock must explore without inhibition the conflicts in his own emotional makeup that illuminate those of "the Jew". My priority then was to get inside the head of Shylock and discover how many of his feelings found their echoes in mine.

I started from where I was, from what I knew, from how I felt about the relationships in the play as I saw them in the moment, without concern about ultimate interpretation of the part or its refinement. The process was like an extended "emotional preparation", a succession of "daydreams", in a manner reminiscent of my work with the great master teacher, Sanford Meisner. But instead of preparing for entrance to a scene, on a subliminal level I sensed I was exploring the depths of Shylock's mind.

Sandy M.'s methods for preparation and improvisation were, as he put it, "an emotional five-finger exercise", with the objective of getting emotional juices flowing in preparation for engaging with a text with no predetermined interpretation. My own variations on these techniques produced moving associations, imagery, and deeply felt emotions relating to Shylock and his condition (and the larger Jewish condition) beyond the realm of spare textual analysis.

The images of which I speak, long residing in the recesses of my mind, were graphic and nightmarish; including depictions of Jewish women being driven naked in the streets by the Nazis; jocular crowds witnessing the lynching and burning of blacks in the South; the indignities visited by howling mobs upon black students integrating into Southern schools; and the unspeakable horrors of the Nazi death camps. These were grotesque inhumanities in my memory that evoked visceral feelings of revulsion and murderous rage – emotions dark, painful, and violent – but indispensable in my view to grasping the mind of an unstable, tormented man driven to cut out the heart of his bigoted persecutor. These extremes, as an actor, I felt free to indulge - indeed obliged to indulge - without inhibition; an exploration that probed far beyond intellectual analysis yielding richer emotional fruit.

I hoped that this emotional preparation would provide a stimulating foundation for the voice, breath, body, and text work to follow – work which I had started years earlier with Kristin Linklater with whom I first explored the role of Shylock and confronted the emotional demands of the part.

I have greatly appreciated the exceptional schools of actor training of Meisner and Linklater which, while different in emphasis and practice, I believe are ultimately compatible and mutually enhancing in effects. In approaching Shylock, I felt that deeply aligning myself emotionally with his history and that of the Jews was imperative as a prelude to engaging the emotional content which Linklater emphasised was embedded in the language of Shakespeare's text and unlocked through her exercises. It was my hope that this hybrid approach would prove mutually reinforcing and of special depth.

Having got this accumulation out into the open in raw form, I then consulted reputable "scholarly" sources to see how my feelings and perceptions compared with commonly accepted historical facts regarding the world of Shylock. Were they merely subjective fantasies with no relation to reality? Or were they justifiable emotionally in terms of real conditions and circumstances?

Sadly, as regards the harsh realities of life, but happily from the standpoint of my understanding and emotional intuition, the historical record regarding the anguish of the Jews confirmed, indeed heightened, the profound outrage pervading my notes: revealing a searing wound at the heart of the Jewish experience without which, in my view, the volatile Shylock cannot resonate or even make much sense in performance.

Putting it mildly, there was good cause for Shylock's emotional excesses, however aberrant they may appear, and it didn't require a historical stretch to explain them. In consequence, I felt that polemic indictment, railing against the crushing abuse of Jewry, was very much at the emotional root of this play and key to understanding the character of Shylock and the dynamics of his relationship with the Christian world around him.

I must admit, it also seemed a mystery to me that anyone wanting to do *MV* in our time would avoid, miss, or downplay the vital centrality of Shylock's persecution and his reaction to it. It heightened my sense of resentment that at this late date, after all we know about the consequences of antisemitism, the play could be cleansed of some of the major elements at the root of its conflict, or that Shylock could be rendered the butt of comedy or derision.

That Shylock's suffering should be viewed as trivial or subordinate to a theme of self-congratulatory Christian allegory seemed to me indefensible and representative of the insensitivity reflected in the play's Venetian characters. Whatever Shakespeare's personal intent may have been in writing the work, his expansive humanity and instinct as a playwright have ensured that Shylock's passion and obsessions reside clearly in the text, close to its surface. They cannot, and indeed must not, be missed.

Therein, my notes suggested, lies the play's true drama and significance. Sermonising about the virtues of "harmony and perfect love" being triumphant over "usury and corrupt love" in a Christian fantasyland[18] became what I saw as a diversion from the core truth of the play.

What emerged from this emotional exploration were feelings unvarnished, "unbalanced", harsh and dramatic, shorn of the diplomatic niceties and constraints normally expected in discussions of Jewish-Christian relations and Shakespeare – protocols to which I normally adhere in "civilian life" as a matter of course. But we are not dealing here with "civilian life" but rather with the experimental blood and guts of the Theatre. And in the words, once again, of Sanford Meisner: "There are no ladies and gentlemen in the theatre!" Civility is not only inhibiting from an acting point of view, but it can mask unhappy truths in life and serve as a façade for emotional cowardice.

And actors, above all, must not be emotional cowards.

Holding cowardice at bay, and with my emotional work fortified by research, I ventured still further into the emotionally dark side of

Western civilisation to better understand the reasons for Shylock's uncivilised behaviour. I did so under no illusion that the results would be diplomatic or pretty. I felt the process must, in fact, be subjective, emotional, messy. I needed the full foundation of a character, however the portrayal might later be refined.

Ultimately, I must admit to the hope that what I've written down may have some literary merit in the bargain. But I am prepared for the prospect that it may violate the proper bounds of both critic and actor: lack of balance or "good taste" in the first instance; excessive revelation of private, internal processes and obsessions in the second.

Yet, my new incarnation as a writer dictates that I violate (reluctantly and uneasily) Meisner's sage advice to the actor regarding emotional preparation: *"If anyone asks you how you got that [your emotional state], tell them, it's none of your Goddamn business!!"*

Thus, the weighty charge of the actor who wants to undertake the part of Shylock and divorce himself from its prejudicial historical baggage is to find a modern, compelling motivation to make Shylock's excesses believable in modern terms and to explore without inhibition the most painful dimensions of life to serve that end.

The approach I've described reflects personal choices that had resonance for me. Other possibilities are as diverse as the actors who make them and may encompass a range of experiences far removed from the given circumstances of the play. The only imperative is that the choices made bring life to a character in the eyes of an audience (who should have no inkling of the sources drawn upon).

And to quote my mentor again: "You know what moves you."

Irony

In the closing chapter of *Shylock: A Legend and Its Legacy*, John Gross[19] sets out contending arguments of those critics who embrace the traditional (or neo-traditional) view of *MV* as a work of Christian allegory and fantasy to be read on a prima facie basis, and those who contend that the work be viewed in a more realistic contemporary sense as "ironic" with the expressed values of its characters belied by their actual behaviour.

My approach to *MV* sees it as hyper-ironic in view of the marked disparity between the moral pretensions of its leading characters and their degrading behaviour towards Shylock. My belief is that art is not an isolated abstraction with no consequences but, rather, a dynamic component of social reality with effects that must be considered. And I believe productions of *MV* should not be approached without cognisance of the moral implications attendant to it in our time.

The fact that antisemitism was woven into the fabric of the Christian society of Shakespeare's day must not be allowed to recommend it in our own, especially in light of where those tendencies have led. Moreover, the brilliance of Shakespeare's writing only compounds the problem, especially in the wake of the enormity of the Holocaust, by associating Shakespeare's name with the chronic history of anti-Jewish prejudice that led to it. For the image of Shylock the demonic Jew became a staple of European antisemitism for centuries before the Holocaust; an association made the more pointed by *MV*'s status as a popular and frequently produced play in Nazi Germany itself.[20]

Therefore, the two-fold questions we face are which of these alternatives – "prima facie" or "ironic" – best reflects Shakespeare's true intention, and whether the two are in fact mutually exclusive, i.e., whether the most poetic and high-status of *MV*'s characters can be both noble and high-minded on the one hand while hypocritical and bigoted on the other.

I would contend that *prima facie vs. ironic* is neither a "zero-sum game" nor an "either/or" proposition. To conceptualise it as such is a false dichotomy that flies in the face of human experience. Contradiction is at the root of the human condition and manifests at levels high and low throughout history. No one, however well-intentioned, operates purely based on "admirable ideals", nor are such values or their ironic opposites consistently demonstrated.

One of the most eloquent advocates of the "Rights of Man", Thomas Jefferson, is thought to have had a slave mistress – a most "ironic" contradiction, indeed, if true, but one which doesn't discredit his high ideals however much it may call into question the integrity of his personal conduct. People don't go skulking about "indicating" their "irony" and we usually become aware of irony only after the fact, when one set of values and behaviours collide with another and are viewed from a distance.

Consequently, the fact that the sentiments of Portia or Bassanio, or even Antonio, do not "feel" ironic at any given moment, as suggested by John Gross, doesn't contradict the fact that they are ironic when viewed in a larger context. Unthinking contradictions are the very source of their irony, and *the more unpremeditated the thought, the more heightened the effect.*

I would argue that how we view a character or assess a writer and their work is not a one-dimensional question. It is not simply a matter of skill and originality divorced from the nature of the artist and their creation. At times a tense relationship may exist between them which affects our feelings as well. Art divorced from morality can produce a disturbing cognitive dissonance profoundly affecting our sensibilities. Great talent in the service of debased values is the more perverse for its greatness. And how we judge Shakespeare's place and that of *MV* in these deliberations is particularly troubling.

Insofar as *MV*'s characters are concerned, irony appears not only possible among the "beautiful people" of Venice or London but – given the proclivities of this social elite – highly likely.

The Revengers: Murder Most Foul or Poetic Justice?

> *"I have killed a man. But I am not a murderer."*
> (Soghomon Tehlirian, assassin of Talaat Pasha,
> architect of the Armenian genocide)

Our perception of Shylock hinges critically upon our assessment of his condition and his motivations. Is he a perverse, hate-filled, even demonic individual intent upon victimising the Christians around him without cause, or is he a profoundly abused victim of those Christians – driven to retribution in extremis? And to what extent are his extremes found in the experience of other victims of historical abuse, whose deadly excesses were at least deemed understandable if not morally justified?

The proscription against killing as commonly understood in the English-speaking world is based upon a mistranslation of the Ten Commandments which says in the original Hebrew, "Do not Murder" (לֹא תִּרְצָח/Lo Tirzach) – with murder defined as the premeditated killing of an innocent person. This does not rule out in the Jewish tradition or the Christian one the act of killing for just cause – personal or national defence for example. The act of murder, moreover, is a crime according to Jewish law that God himself puts beyond redemption in this life since He allows forgiveness on Yom Kippur (The Day of Atonement) only for offences against himself and against others for which the offender has demonstrated true repentance and received forgiveness from his victim. Obviously, by God's own decree, this is impossible in the case of murder.

From the earliest days of human history, however, murder has been a common practice and moral failing of humankind. Yet there are certain circumstances, morally "grey areas", as in the case of certain assassinations, in which the object of murder is judged to be so malevolent as to make the act seem palatable or even just. Shakespeare himself alludes to this in the murder of Julius Caesar, which after much internal debate Brutus considers to be imperative in defence of a free Republic. And Hamlet is encouraged by the ghost of his father to seek revenge and retribution against his murderer uncle – an act which he ultimately pursues despite fears of godly retribution and his own personal ambivalence.

In the modern era, we have seen many acts of political violence, some petty, some perverse, and some evoking a sense of poetic justice.

In the 1920s two such cases involved the assassination of political figures deemed guilty of the mass murder of Armenians and Jews. The first in 1921 was the assassination in Berlin of Talaat Pasha, the former Grand Vizier of the Ottoman Empire, at the hands of Soghomon Tehlirian, an agent of *Operation Nemesis* – an organised plan of retribution of the Armenian Revolutionary Federation against Ottoman officials deemed responsible for the Armenian genocide during WWI. This atrocity took the lives of 1.2-1.5 million people including 85 members of Tehlirian's own family.

On March 15, 1921 – in Berlin's Charlottenburg district where he had taken up residence – Tehlirian stalked Taalat Pasha, the architect of the persecution, shot him at close range and waited for the police to arrest him. His trial became a sensation and his defence a cause célèbre among those sympathetic to the Armenian cause and that of human rights. When asked about his feelings at trial, Tehlirian declared: "I do not consider myself guilty because my conscience is clear…I have killed a man. But I am not a murderer". The jury clearly agreed and found him "not guilty" in slightly over an hour.

A second and very similar case was that of Sholem Schwartzbard, a Yiddish poet, revolutionary, and veteran of the French Foreign Legion and the International Brigade of the Red Guard living in exile in Paris. During the civil war in Russia, he personally witnessed the devastation wrought by White Russian and Ukrainian nationalist forces and the pogroms they inflicted upon the Jewish populations of Ukraine with estimates of over 100,000 deaths, including 15 members of Schwartzbard's family in Odesa.

Symon Petliura, head of the Directorate of the Ukrainian National Republic, was widely held responsible for these atrocities, and upon discovering that Petliura had fled Ukraine and taken up residence in Paris, Schwartbard resolved to unilaterally administer justice. Here again, as with Tehlirian, he plotted and tracked the movements of his target, confronted him on a street of the Latin Quarter in Paris, shot him multiple times, and waited for the police to arrive. Upon being arrested, he declared: "I have killed a great assassin".

The 1927 trial of Schwartzbard was also a cause célèbre involving one of the most celebrated defence attorneys of the period, the radical lawyer Henri Torres who placed great emphasis on the barbarity of the pogroms which impelled Schwartbard's violence. Torres declared:

> My conclusion was short. I evoked the French Revolution about which no living person could say that he has not inherited something from it: 'Let this man be free who bears on his forehead the stigma of the tragedy of a People!' You hold today in your hands, Members of the Jury, the prestige of this Nation and the destiny of thousands of human lives that is attached to the verdict of France. If I had not been heard, France would have been no longer France and Paris would have been no longer Paris.

After 35 minutes of deliberation, Sholem Schwartbard was acquitted.[21]

The Heart of the Problem

The most daunting problem for the actor playing Shylock is that of discovering his motivation for taking the "pound of flesh". This grisly objective is at the heart of the play's conflict and the source and reflection of its antisemitism, for it imputes to "the Jew" either a pathological mind at work or a racial animus so profound as to go beyond all civilised bounds. The play presents no evidence of the former, and a great many assumptions, without foundation, of the latter.

While Shylock does declare, "I hate him for he is a Christian...*etc.*", his animosity hardly rises to the level of homicide let alone sadism, and nothing in the play suggests previously aberrant behaviours that would lead in that direction.

Although Shylock initially proposes the "pound of flesh" bargain at the crux of the conflict, it is clear from the outset that there is an element of cynicism and unreality in the gesture. Throughout the scene – despite clear feelings of resentment towards Antonio – Shylock repeatedly tries to ingratiate himself with the man, to accommodate him, to elicit some glimmer of respect and comity from him.

The suggestion made by some that his proposal is a brazenly malevolent attempt to lure Antonio into a deadly trap seems highly dubious on the face of it and without plausible justification. The proposal is bizarre, of questionable legality, likely unenforceable, and is dismissed by Shylock himself as worthless to him: *"A pound of man's flesh taken from a man, is not so estimable, profitable neither as flesh of muttons, beefs, or goats ... " (1.3)*.

Antonio, for his part, doesn't take it seriously either. Lured by the prospect of "easy money", and overly confident of his expected profits then at sea, he rejects Bassanio's misgivings about the agreement rather blithely. And its acceptance by Antonio is indicative in Shylock's mind of nothing more than the perverse stupidity of the "goyim". No suspicion of malevolent intent is foreshadowed initially, except for the momentary qualms of Bassanio that are quickly put to rest by Antonio himself.

When we first meet Shylock, he seems little more than a man of the Rialto – preoccupied with business, daily profit and loss, and little else – hardly a murderer in waiting ready to pounce. He has his resentments to be sure – it's not as though he's treated with the greatest respect by the Christians around him, especially Antonio – but he makes the effort to ingratiate himself and deal with them, nonetheless. Why then is it accepted, uncritically, that his sudden and violent impulse to homicidal mutilation is plausible absent the most severe provocation unless one assumes the perversity, moral depravity, and inherent evil of "the Jew" as a given?

As it happens, Christian society of the day was rife with just such assumptions and imagery, ranging from deicide to blood libel (the ritual murder of Christian children and the drinking of Christian blood). And I would contend that a proper understanding of the play's meaning in its time cannot be divorced from these assumptions implicit in the text and undoubtedly present in the minds of its original audience. Moreover, it is imperative to note the cruel irony (though most often overlooked) that these grotesque libels are the very antithesis of Jewish law (Halacha) which views as abomination not only murder but even the mutilation of a corpse, let alone a living being, human or animal. Thus, a serious proposition involving the forfeit of "a pound of flesh" would be anathema to a believing Jew.

Contrast this, if you will, to the prevailing norms of Christendom, where the rack, boiling oil, drawing and quartering, and all manner of perverted desecrations of living flesh were presented as public spectacle presided over by clergy. Shylock could not have been oblivious to this reality nor unmoved by it.

So, when Shylock finally demands his "pound of flesh" is he not confronting the Christian world with its own debasement and hypocrisy? He demands his bond by their standards not his own and questions the integrity of their highest legal institutions if they don't comply with his demands. By Jewish standards such a transaction would be unthinkable, but Shylock declares, in effect, as the pop saying goes, *"it's your world, I only live in it! … So, you 'goyishe' bastards, pay up!"*

Ignoring this context relegates Shylock to the level of caricature, of antisemitic Grand Guignol, and presents us with a figure embodying totally unmotivated evil and blood libel. The fact that such evil is comfortably invested in the image of "the Jew" as opposed to any number of other groups with more substantial records of real-life flesh-carving is telling and inescapable. No one familiar with the history of Christian society of that period can claim that this choice was inadvertent or inconsequential, or that it can be overlooked today.

"Hath Not a Jew Eyes", Indeed!

I would propose that Shakespeare's nagging neutrality on the question of prescription vs. description regarding his characters suggests the very means by which to counter the antisemitic traditions of *MV* in his own words. For it must be recognised that a strange contradiction exists between the bigoted view of Shylock as unalloyed miscreant and villain undeserving of sympathy or respect, and the words of Shakespeare himself. In perhaps the most eloquent, moving, and best-known speech of the play – Shylock's *"Hath not a Jew eyes?"* speech – Shakespeare provides a telling riposte to the calumnies directed towards Shylock.

While not a plea for tolerance as some would wish it to be, the *"Hath not a Jew eyes?"* speech is, nonetheless, a powerful and strikingly ironic claim of common humanity between Jew and Christian based upon a common and all too human penchant for revenge! To deny this moral equation – based upon a propensity for violence so common in Shakespeare's day – is to assume that Jews occupy an inferior moral universe vis à vis Christians; a universe so debased as to put them beyond all claims of equity, something which Shakespeare, by the agency of this most famous speech, clearly does not do. Why, then, is his point not taken?

Thus, the conundrum regarding Shakespeare's true intent is shrouded in contradictions and finds no simple answer. While *MV* shows clear evidence of perversely antisemitic attitudes endemic to the Christian society of Shakespeare's day and centuries thereafter, Shakespeare's personal views remain in doubt.

The Jewish Question and the Lure of Anachronism

Why is Shylock a Jew? Why not an Armenian, Greek, Arab, Turk, or Italian Christian for that matter – all of whom could be found in trade and, possibly, usury? Is the choice merely incidental and inconsequential, or is there a pejorative reason for it?

The plot of *MV* is strikingly close to the collection of fifty short stories, *Il Pecorone* by the 14th century Italian author, Ser Giovanni Fiorentino, but Shakespeare's motivation for using these themes is not clear. His thinking on this subject remains a mystery but his choice suggests that antisemitic themes were already established and popular in European culture for centuries and apparently "box office" in his time as well, to which *MV* and *The Jew of Malta* attest.

Moreover, once having retained a Jewish moneylender as a pivotal part of the drama, why continue to attribute to him, as Fiorentino did, a scheme involving homicidal mutilation? Is this just a matter of happenstance, reluctance to part from the original source, or is there a larger motivation behind it specific to Shakespeare and his times? I would argue that to accept uncritically this peculiar confluence of ethnic and ghoulish elements in *MV* is intellectually myopic and indefensible, especially in our time.

Some who are eager to downplay the overtly antisemitic implications of these choices will argue that Shylock's status as a Jew is inconsequential, that *MV* should be viewed more generically as a universal statement unrelated to distinct ethnic prejudice. But are we to believe that it is possible to set up social, religious, or ethnic minorities as grotesques and then credibly assert they are there to represent universal truths common to all humanity? The minority (ethnic or religious) is an "exotic", a foreigner, the "other" (and this was truer of Elizabethan times than our own). In an age characterised more by xenophobia than inclusion, Shylock's travails could not be readily expected to inspire sympathy in the minds of an Elizabethan audience. Derision was the most likely possibility – a fact that must not be lost on us today.

There is great danger here of being culturally anachronistic, attributing insights and sensitivities to past generations that are relatively recent accretions of our own, however imperfectly realised. It may well be that Shakespeare foreshadowed the enlightenment of ages yet to come – it is a satisfying notion to believe that he did – but that is by no means certain, and it is highly doubtful that his audiences possessed that degree of enlightenment even if he did.

We must be aware, therefore, of how easily our own thinking may slip unsuspectingly into anachronism. While some in our time intent on absolving *MV* of charges of antisemitism may suggest that Shakespeare proposes moral equity for Shylock, we must not blithely assume that Elizabethan audiences perceived it that way. Shylock's claims to equity could easily have been viewed by them with distain – as a grotesque joke to be dismissed out of hand as patently ridiculous.

Just as similar appeals by Southern blacks would have been ridiculed by the racist Southern whites around them.

The bigoted mind has myriad ways to blind itself to even the most compelling claims of humanity if it wishes, as was no doubt the case when *MV* was viewed by Nazi audiences for whom it was hugely popular. It would be absurd to suppose that Nazi attitudes towards Jews were in any way softened by the theatrical experience.[22]

Thus, the conundrum remains regarding Shakespeare's true intent, as does the reason to pay close attention to precisely how *MV* is interpreted and to what end it is used today. For that reason, unorthodox questions must be asked, and reconsideration of old assumptions and relationships must be made.

Shylock and Antonio

> *"The last temptation is the greatest treason*
> *To do the right deed for the wrong reason."*
> (T.S. Eliot, Murder in the Cathedral)

Antonio is presented as one of the most overtly antisemitic of the play's characters on the one hand, while being touted as an exemplar of selfless love and Christian virtue on the other. To the Elizabethan and traditional Christian mind this was doubtless unexceptional and implied no contradiction.

Antonio's apparent "selflessness" in lending money "gratis" – much to the consternation of Shylock – is cited by traditionalists as a statement of profound Christian ideals and elevated sensibilities, in comparison to Shylock whose entire life revolves around debased materialism and the corrupt practice of lending money for profit. But his "charity" may not be what it seems.

That modern critical opinion can seriously entertain this perspective in the wake of the Protestant Reformation and the last few centuries of Western capitalist development is quite extraordinary. I would guess that those persisting in such illusions were so protected from reality by British class privilege as to sustain a medieval Christian fantasy world of their own.

What is the implication vis à vis Shylock of Antonio's much-lauded practice of lending money "gratis"? Rather than a sign of "grace and generosity of spirit", is it not a vindictive provocation (in the words of *Monty Python*) of an upper-class "twit" sufficiently wealthy and well-placed to toy maliciously and with impunity with the fortunes of a legitimate businessman? And is there not a perverse pleasure in exercising such faux generosity at the expense of the "avaricious Jew"?

Shylock's livelihood and that of his family depends upon his profits as with all business professionals. Where is the "justice" in frivolously denying him that? (By the way, such behaviour is explicitly forbidden to Jews by Halacha – Jewish religious law – which prevents Jewish merchants from cornering a market to the extent that livelihood is denied to a competitor. So much for "superior" notions of Christian "charity"). As his behaviour demonstrates, Antonio does not even do so for personal gain – by virtue of his position he doesn't need to – but rather for overtly spiteful, antisemitic reasons, with no small amount of unctuous posturing for public consumption into the bargain.

Yet, despite this history of class antagonism, we are still left with the nagging question of proportion running through the play. Shylock's hatred and desire for revenge seem excessive as does the spiteful, seemingly unmotivated, malevolence of Antonio towards him. The antagonism seems instinctive rather than rational but must be understood if the extremity of their mutual hate is to make sense in human and dramatic terms. Is there perhaps a profound and unstated psychological source for this antagonism of an existential nature?

Antonio and Bassanio

> *"Thou shalt not lie with mankind, as with womankind:*
> *it is abomination." (Leviticus, 18:22)*
> וְאֶת־זָכָר לֹא תִשְׁכַּב מִשְׁכְּבֵי אִשָּׁה תּוֹעֵבָה הִוא׃

The relationship between Antonio and Bassanio presents interesting questions that have implications for the Shylock-Antonio relationship at the heart of the play. Traditionally, it has been interpreted as a symbol of altruism and platonic Christian love, standing in contrast to the self-serving materialism of "the Jew".

More recently, however, in line with changing cultural norms, Antonio's devotion has been seen as suggesting a homosexual passion for Bassanio; with this passion being at the root of his melancholy and selfless generosity towards his friend. Several major productions in recent years have approached the Antonio-Bassanio relationship in this way.[23] But none has ventured beyond that to explore the possible implications of this choice regarding the conflict between Antonio and Shylock.

A gay Antonio of the period might likely view Shylock as emblematic of an Old Testament reproach of his very being. Indeed, latent homosexuality (or not so latent as the case may be) might play a potent role in explaining Antonio's seemingly unmotivated yet chronic hostility towards Shylock and the vehemence of it.[24]

Shylock, by virtue of who he is, strikes at the heart of the merchant's innermost self. Antonio knows it and his only effective response under the circumstances is to use his social advantages to delegitimate "the Jew", which he does with a vindictiveness unmatched by any of his peers. Moreover, Antonio's hostility and "vice" are not lost on Shylock and, arguably, add to his rage at being treated so indignantly by an individual symbolic in his mind of the decadent "abominations" he associates with the Christian world.

Thus, the stage is set for an unstated existential antagonism that makes the stakes more nearly require a "pound of flesh" on both sides. An antagonism between the patriarchal, heterosexual, unyielding, monotheistic God of Old Testament Judaism; and the paganised, victimised, polytheized, feminised deity of New Testament Christianity,[25,26] and the Roman (read "decadent") Church that worships Him. For both parties, there can be no compromise between these two positions. Once the lines have been drawn and the battle engaged, Shylock must get his "bond" – or Venice must convert "the Jew" and make him "kiss the cassock".

In addition, the directorial choice of an intimate Antonio-Bassanio relationship could suggest a rather mercenary dimension to the character of the romantic Bassanio and call into question the transactional nature of their relationship – i.e., love for love or love for money?

The implications of this clandestine coupling could reverberate further still, subverting the image of pure love attributed to Bassanio and the virtuous Portia. A complication potentially clouding their idyllic relationship in an unknown future – a prospect she might first have hint of only at play's end.

Thus, the "pure love" of *MV* could end on a hanging question of "what is love and for how long?" – a further dimension of un-Christian hypocrisy added to the main characters and the world of Belmont they inhabit with pregnant questions for the future.

Whatever the merits of this approach to the Antonio-Bassanio relationship and the romantic entanglements attendant to it, the choice of a gay Antonio at the least provides another level of potent antagonism between the merchant and the moneylender, Shylock – an animosity of some dramatic utility even if many would be inclined to avoid it.

Shylock and Portia

If we are concerned with the hypocrisy and the malevolence of the Venetians towards Shylock – and I think we should be – nowhere are these offences more painfully manifest than in the conduct of the play's most vaunted figure, Portia. This may seem a shocking comment, but consider the following:

In the trial scene (4.1) Portia intervenes in the guise of a Doctor of Laws named Balthazar, supposedly sent by an esteemed Doctor of Laws in Padua, Bellario, for the purpose of defending Antonio. Nowhere in the play is there any reference to a previous relationship or encounter between Portia and Shylock, whose respective worlds do not coincide. Moreover, she opens her interrogation by asking: "Which is the merchant here and which the Jew?"

Whether this query is truly meant or part of her disguise as a foreign magistrate from Padua is open to conjecture but, suffice to say, it doesn't suggest a previous connection between them. Portia then proceeds to mount a vigorous and deft defence of Antonio by first trying to dissuade Shylock from pursuing his case against him by means of the most sympathetic and moving speech, *"The quality of mercy is not strained…"* – an appeal that falls on deaf ears as far as it pertains to Shylock.

This speech is a beautiful sentiment and supposed evidence of the elevated moral stature and sensibilities of the Christian side of the equation (and a favourite of young actors wanting to portray refined emotional depth).

But is it really?

Many are invested emotionally in the belief that Portia's virtues are eloquently demonstrated by her lecture to Shylock. But her subsequent behaviour at the trial's end calls these assumptions into question.

To begin with, there is no indication that Portia has ever

demonstrated the mercy she so eloquently advocates towards anyone, least of all Shylock. Right from the start she refers to him in crudely ethnic terms lacking the simplest honorific or element of courtesy expected in court proceedings – a propensity for racism reflected in contempt for her black suitor, Morocco, and "all of his complexion", in the casket scene (3.3), as well. And after mounting a deft defence of Antonio and beating Shylock on the merits, is she "mercifully" satisfied with his capitulation?

Not in the least!

She presses even more zealously onto the attack to destroy him utterly – denying him the return of his loan to Antonio, and destroying what remains of his business, money, possessions and his religion.

In short, Portia becomes the wielder of the shiv which she plunges in and twists! And all this as prelude to the play's "happy ending".

Some mercy!

Portia's refined vindictiveness and cruelty, however stately and articulate, could not be more apparent; and yet is hidden in plain sight in the minds of many who, for reasons of their own pretensions to refinement and higher sensibilities, are loath to see them.

Portia's Realm: Belmont as Bloomsbury

World of Fantasy, World of Exclusion

Belmont is seen, traditionally, as something of a fairyland, an enchanted realm that is the home of a woman "fair" and of "wondrous virtues" – the aforementioned Portia – the "fairy queen" of the realm, as it were. It serves as the embodiment and highest reflection of Venice's Christian society in contrast to the debasement of the Rialto and its Jewish denizen, Shylock. Truth, beauty, and refinement are its credo, together with a happy sense of mischief and frivolity unavailable to the "less deserving" classes of society. To those who pay little heed to the larger implications of the play and its unfortunate abuse of "the Jew" the institution of Belmont serves as a delightful diversion, offering a vision of grace and amorousness that is greatly appealing.

But I would suggest there is a darker side to Belmont beneath the surface; an environment of fatuousness, self-indulgence, self-obsession, and self-interest that blinds its inhabitants to the realities of the world around them and that, in the story as considered here, highlights the insensitivity and injustice being perpetrated against Shylock, "the Jew". I would venture to say that this dynamic parallels to a considerable degree the character of Britain's presence in an array of developing countries during her period of empire and most assuredly describes the oblivion and outright callousness of British policy towards the Jews and their plight during the war years and their aftermath in Palestine.

When Belmont is seen from the perspective of its class privilege, distance from the real world, and the insensitivities that flow from them, Portia's "superior wisdom" at trial regarding "the quality of mercy" takes on a wholly different and hypocritical light. Thus, the most sympathetic and seemingly refined character in the play, seemingly possessed of all the virtues, can be seen as tainted by the same bigoted worldview regarding "the Jew" as her compatriots are. And this is a telling indictment if effectively made in performance.

There was a modern setting in Britain which exhibited many of these characteristics and which might prove useful as a point of reference and social model for the vision of Belmont I would propose; that is, the collection of intellectuals, writers, artists, and aesthetes that became known as the Bloomsbury Group or Set. A rather more intellectual and culturally weighty crowd than that suggested by the original Belmont, they nonetheless were distinguished by a lifestyle studiously at odds with social norms, proclivity for "unconventional" sexual mores and liaisons, and a predominant tone of frivolity, badinage, and self-obsession largely untroubled by the ominous upheavals of the pre-war years.[27]

"The acceptance of erotic license and hostility towards social convention"[28] characteristic of Bloomsbury and its extremes – including some casual upper-class antisemitism on the part of some of its members – coupled with the overt antisemitism reflected in *MV* are elements I would combine in de-mythologising the image of Belmont and its function in the interpretation suggested here. British imperialism created a vast network of Belmonts that functioned in blithe disregard of the squalor and deprivation of the native peoples around them, denying their humanity much as the play's characters deny that of Shylock, "the Jew".

Shylock and Blood Libel: The Unkindest Cut of All?

> *"I took by th' throat the circumcised dog*
> *And smote him thus."*
> (Othello, 5.2.341-354)

The issue of circumcision seems linked to *MV* in a variety of unsavoury ways. First as an element of blood libel lurking at the root of the play's conflict and second as a sadistic element in depiction of the character Shylock. The malevolent role played by blood libel and circumcision in the minds of the Elizabethans and the persistence of such imagery in modern society, despite widespread acceptance of the practice for medical reasons, calls for examination.

The "circumcised dog" referred to contemptuously by Othello (5.2) was in fact a Muslim Turk not a Jew, but the derisive inclusion of circumcision as a pejorative in Shakespeare's text suggests an established prejudice of significance in his day. Moreover, reference to a circumcised Turk as a "dog" is an insult hurled at Shylock as well

(*"You call me misbeliever, cutthroat dog, and spit upon my Jewish gabardine…"*, and again, in the same speech, *"You, that did void your rheum upon my beard and foot me as you spurn a stranger cur over your threshold."* (*MV* 1.3.103-126)). No doubt these ethnic slurs, redolent with bloody sexual overtones and bestial allusions, were resonant in the minds of Elizabethan audiences well-accustomed to the blood libels that stigmatised Jews as detested and perverted aliens. Resonance that echoes in several guises to this day.

An example of this mindset was demonstrated some years ago – rather graphically – in a short documentary preceding a production of *MV* on *PBS*, in which the actor playing Shylock was directed to approach Antonio menacingly in the trial scene with knife unsheathed; suggestive, in the director's words, of the act of circumcision! And the director was serious! When I first saw this I was appalled, thinking him oblivious to the profoundly offensive implication of comparing what to the observant Jew and Muslim is a symbol of their covenant with God, to an act of homicidal mutilation.

But I have since come to discover that the view of circumcision as an act of sanguinary violence was not the director's creation nor limited to medieval prejudices. It finds its origins in a convoluted path of theological imagery and rhetoric stretching from benign Old Testament references to "circumcision" in a euphemistic sense, suggesting sanctification of the heart and lips in addition to a physical symbol of Israel's covenant with God, to Paul's "displacement" of the concept from the "physical to the spiritual and of the flesh by … the heart."[29] The latter became a foundation stone of Christian doctrine and an important point of departure of early Christians from their Jewish forebears. The concepts of Christian supersession and Jewish displacement became increasingly and aggressively antisemitic over time affecting Christian attitudes and literature, medieval and modern.[30]

Thus, we see a strange and tortuous mutation of the concept of circumcision: from a physical symbol of Israel's covenant with God, to Pauline Christianity's "circumcision of the heart"; followed by the hostile and distorted notion – meant no doubt to further discredit the Jewish version – that physical circumcision is to be thought of in league with castration. And the shorthand equation, circumcision=castration, comes to be seen as the basis of Shylock's motivation and character.

This distortion is not limited to medieval thinking, however. Similar concepts are found in modern secular terms as well, in the writings of Sigmund Freud and his analyst disciple Theodore Reik – sources from which, I suspect, the director may have taken his cue. Reik carries Pauline "displacement" still further in his analysis of *MV* by asserting that Shylock, subconsciously, substitutes the heart for the "member" as the site of his "cutting" (a curious transference when you stop to think of it since Shylock is obviously not Christian and would not be inclined to perceive things in Pauline Christian terms, much less modern psychoanalytic ones). Thus, Reik renders Shylock's bond "... a substitute expression of castration" which leads, one suspects, to the kind of directorial choice mentioned above.

It is shocking to me how redolent this modern psychoanalytic assessment is to the superstitious blood libels that preceded it for centuries, conflating in medieval fashion circumcision with castration and suggesting that Shylock's demand to extract the "pound of flesh" reflects the paradoxical desire to castrate his adversary while transforming him into a "Jew".[31]

It was a staple of medieval blood libels that Jews were accused of "turning Christians Jew" by forcefully circumcising them before crucifying them, ritually murdering them, draining their blood for ritual purposes, and cannibalising the remains.[32] It apparently never occurred to the Christian minds of the period that the putative "gratification" to be derived by Jews in allegedly misusing their

Christian victims in this way might be seriously compromised by first "turning them Jew", as it were. But facts and logic have never been antisemitism's strong suit.[33]

The great 17th-century Rabbi Menasseh ben Israel made just this point in his *Vindiciae Judaeorum*, in defence of the Jew's return to England under Oliver Cromwell, in which he repudiated the ritual-murder canard, declaring: "If it was intended that shortly after this child should be crucified, to what end was he first circumcised?"[34] One can only look with horror upon any remnant of this notion surviving in our modern age and culture, especially after the Holocaust which saw it drawn upon and amplified a thousandfold.

I suspect that because of these scholarly influences the director in question, whom I understand to be a man of liberal sympathies who went to some lengths to explain Shylock's plight, accepted such symbolism as fair game and within the bounds of propriety. And based upon interviews with him I am sure he would be appalled to think he had committed a faux pas let alone an act of antisemitism. But in a sense that is just my point. As stated at the outset, interpreting *MV* really is "a virtual litmus test".

Even more appalling is the deliberate reversion to blood libel tropes vis à vis circumcision by modern, sophisticated, and ostensibly "progressive" intellectuals. One such was the late author Christopher Hitchens, an avowed atheist, who in his zeal to disparage Old Testament Judaism shockingly resorted to humour redolent of Medieval blood libel. His oft-repeated admonition trotted out unashamedly at public gatherings, sometimes jocularly, sometimes with vituperation and derision, "Never buy crackling from a Mohel!" – suggesting that Rabbis would fry the foreskin remains of circumcision and sell them for human consumption – was a disgusting mockery with no relevance to the question of circumcision pro or con that should have been beneath a man of his intellect.[35] Nonetheless, it was a barb he employed repeatedly and without shame in public gatherings which is, perhaps, not surprising given the fact that Britain first originated the concept of blood libel, including cannibalism, directed against the Jews and was the first European country to expel its Jewish population.

Yet the 92nd Street Y where Hitchens spoke on several occasions proved a receptive audience, which suggests that an Oxbridge accent and the upper-crust status it confers can excuse all offenses in the minds of sycophantic American anglophiles.

"The Hated Rival"

> *"Since the Jew is nowhere at home, nowhere regarded as a native, he remains an alien everywhere. That he himself and his ancestors as well are born in the country does not alter this fact in the least…to the living the Jew is a corpse, to the native a foreigner, to the homesteader a vagrant, to the proprietary a beggar, to the poor an exploiter and a millionaire, to the patriot a man without a country, for all a hated rival."*
> (Leon Pinsker, Autoemancipation, 1882)

In considering Shylock's behaviour there tends to be an inadequate appreciation of the adverse conditions facing the Jews of medieval and early modern Europe. Many even highly educated and aware people may be cognisant of past discrimination as an abstraction but the image of the hate-filled crowd, the violent mob, or even the grudging, disrespectful acquaintance whose daily "whips and scorns" define the life and self-image of a despised minority has no currency for them. Nor, in most cases, do contemporary Christians grasp the perverted nature of the antisemitic stereotypes that prevailed in Europe for most of its history or comprehend its destructiveness. Shameful bigotries that can still be found in the cultural backwaters of Christendom to this day.[36]

In contemporary society, some people like Jews, some don't, and most are indifferent, but it is only at the extreme margins of society, where indifference or acceptance had never been the case anyway, that a Jewish person would be confronted by overt and violent prejudice (a degree of tolerance suddenly threatened by the horrid Hamas attacks of 07/10/2023 and their aftermath). For past generations, this degree of tolerance was not the case, hostility (overt or covert) was the norm. My own grandmother spoke of a time within living memory when pogroms and intimidation at the hands of Czarist authorities and drunken peasants encouraged in their bigotry by an arch-reactionary Czar and Russian Orthodox Church were the order of the day and a part of her life – and this mere prelude to the unspeakable atrocities of the Holocaust to come.

Medieval and Renaissance societies, while less capable technologically than modern totalitarian states of inflicting mass murder upon hapless populations, were nonetheless prodigious – within their limitations – in doing just that, uninhibited by concepts of universal human rights. Moreover, the Christianity of the period, deeply infused with demonic imagery of the Jew as "Christ-killer", "spawn of Satan", "ritual murderer of children", and "blood-drinker", among other "idiosyncrasies", did little to enlighten or dissuade such tendencies unless the disruptions became sufficiently acute to threaten public order generally or the authority of Church and State.

Thus, a proper grasp of Shylock's emotional state requires a full understanding of the bigotries of traditional Christian society and the destructive effects these abuses would have had upon him. And it is important in this regard to understand the pervasiveness of the anti-Jewish prejudice of the period, the depth of its degradation and its effects psychologically upon the behaviour of its victims.

To start with, in the Romanised Pauline Christian mind, the Jews were the "killers of Christ", and it has taken the better part of two thousand years of Western civilisation for a departure from this canard to be embraced by the Church, its institutions, and its followers. Were this the only slander perpetrated by Christendom against the Jewish People it would have been burden enough given the penchant for violence and vindictiveness that characterised Christian behaviours even towards each other. But the Christian mind found an outlet for its social, economic, political, and even sexual anxieties in further misuse of the Jews over the centuries.

The Jew in the medieval world was seen by Christians as embodying a wide range of perversions, ranging from the demonic to the physically repulsive.[37] Along with the epithets mentioned above, they were viewed as "host desecrators", "well poisoners", "carriers of disease", "economic and political manipulators" and seen as a perpetual threat to Christendom which, according to Christian belief, they wished to abuse and ultimately destroy out of their inveterate hatred for Jesus Christ and his followers.[38]

In addition, they were considered to have an inherently foul odour which was intrinsic to their race; one of several physical curses inflicted upon them because of their rejection and abuse of Jesus. This foul dysfunction was further compounded by the emasculating belief that Jewish men menstruated and as a result required the ingestion of blood to make up for their sanguinary deficiencies which they then pursued by way of the "ritual-murder" of Christian children and adults – fulfilling, simultaneously, their alimentary needs and perverted religious rites.[39]

Such beliefs appear so ludicrous to us today that it is often difficult to take them seriously or to think that they could have had any impact or consequence in their time. But in fact, they were taken very seriously in their time and believed literally; so much so that the victims of these canards could be measured in the displacement or slaughter of whole communities of Jews in Christian Europe throughout the Middle Ages and, unimaginably, in even greater numbers in the modern period as well.

We are faced here with a very telling lacuna in Western moral sensibilities regarding these questions, the abuses being so egregious, frequent, and of such longstanding that they become a commonplace part of the cultural scenery – "Heard, not regarded – seen, but with such eyes as…afford no extraordinary gaze"[40] – abstractions often unremarked, easily ignored, or dispensed with. But is this history not at the very root of Shylock's emotional state and of his relations with the Christians around him? Would his tortured sense of self and animosity towards his offenders not be greatly magnified and aggravated by the larger history of abuse, victimisation, and obloquy to which his people were subjected?

Does no one understand what it means to be told you are not only less than human, but demonic? Does no one grasp the impact on a person's sense of self to be viewed as physically repulsive, inherently, by definition and race? Is there no sensitivity to the corrosive effects over time of defining a group of people as social lepers deserving of exclusion at best or eradication?

What is the effect of living, perpetually, as a hapless minority amid emotional and physical violence and opprobrium with no hope of safe-haven or redress? And at what point do the Shylocks of the world break under the pressure and seek their "pound of flesh"?! Shylock alludes to this history of abuse quite clearly and resentfully in response to Antonio's insults ("still have I borne it with a patient shrug for sufferance is the badge of all our tribe"), and one sees similar tendencies among several contemporary minority groups whose resentments linger past the point of overt aggression on the part of the larger society.

Why then would such effrontery be inconsequential in the mind of someone amid it daily?

Today we can find those who subscribe to negative stereotypes about "the Jews" owning the banks, or the media, or Wall Street or Hollywood. But consider again that in Shakespeare's day it was commonly believed that "the Jews" literally murdered God, slaughtered Christian children, poisoned wells, spread disease, and were biologically unnatural. Owning banks, media outlets, Wall Street brokerages or the movie business is no violation of Jewish religious tenets or those of Christians either, whereas all the former canards of the medieval and early modern eras are grotesque violations of the most important moral precepts of Judaism and Christianity, and the depth of these affronts must be seen as staggering.

* * *

Much is made today of the crippling emotional effects of hostile environments far less extreme than those just described. Yet, when discussions of Shylock are engaged in, suddenly the psychological implications of such abuse are trivialised or overlooked altogether, and the historical slate is wiped clean. Alternatively, the offences are rendered abstract and devoid of emotional impact. If they are not rendered so, the burden of guilt becomes too great for the Christian and the resentment becomes too extreme for the Jew. Life stops in a state of moral and psychological paralysis. Without rationalisation or resolution, avoidance is the only option.

But if we are to understand Shylock, we must engage with a mind that is raw with the immediate pain of this suffering and whose emotional life and behaviour reflect it. Yet, little recognition or understanding is extended to "the Jew" in this regard. Indeed, in Shakespeare's day his role was that of an ogrish foil in a comic motif.

Why is that?

Stereotypes and Consequences

There are a variety of ways that ethnic and racial minorities can be ostracised and dehumanised: in some cases, by crude debasement, in others by a pernicious process of shallow approbation. The former is simply abusive, the latter is both destructive and seductive. In both instances, however, the full humanity of the "other" is denied through a process of stereotyping and abstraction cast in stark shades of black and white (people of colour as drug pushers, pimps and gang members vs. people of colour as athletic superheroes, is a contemporary American example of this). Group members are viewed as cut-outs, not respected as fully rounded human beings possessing strengths, vulnerabilities, virtues, and failings. Their humanity denied they are then consigned to a social nether realm.

The traditional stereotype of Shylock as a villain, usurer, buffoon, and all-purpose, satirical anti-Christ, gave way in the 19th century to a "rehabilitated" version to establish his martyrdom. Both approaches, I submit, are aesthetically and morally inadequate and troubling. To make the "traditional" approach work requires a blind eye to the incontrovertible bigotry of the leading Christian characters in the play while ignoring the humanity of Shylock. Making "martyrdom" work requires ignoring Shylock's manifold prejudices and the extremity of his parochial hatred. In my view, both extremes are not theatrically convincing and produce a vision of dissonance and unreality.

Finally, what do these omissions tell us about the guilt, moral perversity, and insensitivity of some of the West's most cherished beliefs and institutions? It is, perhaps, understandable that the guilty would wish to avoid confronting their guilt, but what excuse do the "enlightened" and liberal-minded have in allowing them to do so? Why do so many cherish the mollifying effects of self-flattery and fantasy – the mentality of Belmont – over the moral responsibility and liberating effects of Truth regarding the condition of Shylock and Jews in general? Is this not what real Christianity – in the true spirit of its Jewish saviour – is supposed to demand?

Injustice can be repudiated. Abuses can be atoned. The downtrodden can be uplifted. Our past failings can be employed to serve the end of future enlightenment. But this cannot be done if we don't choose to do it. I believe that *MV* and Shylock represent iconic symbols of this challenge that demand acknowledgment. Our culture has choices it can make, but engaging in high-tone, high-culture rationalisations and evasions for racial and religious bigotry should not be among them. And this sensibility must inform the interpretation of *MV* and its signature character.

In a certain sense, the words of a great contemporary Jewish playwright – though separated by time and circumstance from the plight of Shylock – has striking resonance here. I refer to what are perhaps the most moving lines in *Death of a Salesman* by Arthur Miller, uttered by Willy Loman's wife, Linda:

> I don't say he's a great man. Willy Loman never made a lot of money. His name was never in the paper. He's not the finest character that ever lived. But he's a human being, and a terrible thing is happening to him. So, attention must be paid. He's not to be allowed to fall into his grave like an old dog. Attention, attention must be finally paid to such a person.[41]

And attention must be paid to Shylock, too.

Shylock as presented in the text may be unattractive but, like Loman, he is also human. He may not be a hero sacrificing himself on the altar of virtue, but he is a man who has been grievously abused. Making him an unalloyed martyr or villain reduces him to caricature and eviscerates the very substantial emotional and dramatic potential of the play. But these are not the only alternatives; nor, do I believe, are they the most interesting ones.

Villain, Martyr, or Everyman?

What strikes me as an intriguing dimension of *MV*, especially considering the world's history since Shakespeare, *is its foreshadowing of dramatic "modernity"; particularly the emergence of the modern anti-hero:* the flawed, inaesthetic, beleaguered "Everyman", who must negotiate his way through an uncaring and unforgiving world and who does so with less than brilliance. This complex and uncathartic "veil of tears" that represents all too often the real condition of humanity speaks to us in a manner that is contemporary, multi-layered, and profound.

Therein, in my view, lies the "truth" of Shylock; a man who would rather have led an uneventful life filled with his own modest triumphs, adversities, and petty obsessions, but is instead thrown into a maelstrom of antagonisms with overtones of Biblical proportions. As stated before, he is "a flawed anti-hero at the end of his tether", not a man transcendent, fitted out for greatness. He deals with the demons around him (and inside him) as best he can *but is inadequate to the task.* He demands "justice" but is denied it. He is "'buked and scorned", as the spiritual says, on every side. He is defeated in the most painful and personal way – loss of daughter, loss of livelihood, loss of religion, loss of self – but still he "goes on" (à la *Waiting for Godot)*. Whether "survival" is his ultimate triumph, or final humiliation, is the unanswered existential question of his life and of our time.

ACTOR'S MEMOIR
Recollections Profound and Profane

"Now that's a *real* antisemite!"

A prominent Anglo-Jewish director and brilliant teacher, Vivian Matalon, once told me a story that dramatises the endemic and persistent character of upper-class antisemitism rather well. He told of being on a cruise where he shared a table at dinner with a wealthy British matron of rather bigoted inclinations. Every evening she made a point of expressing derogatory comments about Jews.

Finally, fed up with this recurring affront, the director, who otherwise had cordial relations with the woman, confronted her and declared, "I really must tell you, Madam, that I find your comments about Jews extremely offensive. I am one myself". To which she replied, imperiously, "Why that's impossible. Of course, you're not!"

The director said to me, "Now that's a *real* antisemite!"

In other words, negative stereotypes of Jews were so thoroughly ingrained in her that she couldn't conceive of anyone to whom she was amicably disposed possibly being part of the "despised race" she felt at liberty to insult.

Conversations with Morris Carnovsky

Upon completing training with Sandy Meisner, I was cast in a production of *The Cherry Orchard* at the Long Wharf Theatre in New Haven, Connecticut. Much to my delight the cast included Morris Carnovsky, a distinguished veteran of The Group Theatre, who played the part of "Firs".

I introduced myself to Morris as a student of Meisner's and we established an immediate rapport (for some reason, which I never fully understood, his presence in the cast seemed of little consequence to the other actors in the production, but for me the continuation of The Group Theatre "connection" was quite exhilarating). During rehearsals, we became fast friends. He relished talking about the Theatre – especially about Stanislavsky – and the breadth of his career and associations read like a theatre history book.

Between rehearsals – in the nearby Howard Johnson's restaurant over hefty plates of strawberry ice cream – Morris held forth on the intricacies of Stanislavsky's method (in which he took a Talmudic interest!) among other topics. At some point, the discussion turned to *MV*, in which he had played a highly regarded Shylock at the *American Shakespeare Festival* in Stratford, Connecticut.

I found Morris, personally, a very kind man and I knew him, politically, to be a man of the Left (in fact, a "named" victim of McCarthy-era blacklisting), and so his expressed quandary in approaching the part of Shylock didn't surprise me.

He said that initially he couldn't fathom the depth of Shylock's hatred of the Christians around him and was at a loss to understand his "motivation" (quite literally). Indeed, Shylock's disposition seemed bigoted and personally distasteful to him and certainly not the image of humane universalism that his own inclinations would have preferred to portray. But, finally, he discovered in the text what he felt to be the key to Shylock's embitterment. According to Morris, it is found in the famous remonstrance to Antonio in 1.3.

There, in two short references that are often given inadequate weight in a larger list of grievances, Shylock reveals that Antonio would "spit" on him. And if that weren't indignity enough, Antonio spat specifically on the very symbols of his Jewishness (*"you call me misbeliever...and you spit upon my Jewish gabardine"*, and yet again, *"You that did void your rheum upon my beard* [a religiously mandated symbol of his identity as a Jew] *and foot me as you spurn a stranger cur over your threshold..."*)

Morris's eyes flashed with intensity. There was the key, he said, to Shylock's hatred, and the reference is made twice in the same speech. He had been humiliated in the crudest and most degrading way publicly, in his place of business, treated like a dog and had been so abused specifically because he was a Jew!

Here was the motivation with which even the most humane-minded leftist of his generation could understand and identify. It was the smouldering resentment of oppressed and humiliated minorities throughout the world towards their overlords and tormentors. It was the resentment of African Americans towards a history of enslavement and "Jim Crow". It was the resentment of the anti-colonialist struggle towards imperialist domination. It was the progressive "hatred" (though the word dares not be uttered) which fuelled "The Revolution" – all revolutions!

Yes, here in the form of an otherwise unattractive and hardly "progressive" figure like Shylock, was this essential "revolutionary" truth: whatever his failings – and they were certainly no worse than those of his detractors – Shylock was an abused, humiliated, and oppressed minority, who responded to his persecutors in a not uncommon way: he hated them! Pure and simple. And if he weren't a Jewish moneylender, the world might even sympathise!

"Out of the mouths of WASPs"

The "crime" of obsession with money is cited as being second only to Shylock's murderous vindictiveness in his character flaws, and justification for distaste of him (as though his critics in the play, not to mention the world at large, are constantly engaged in more "spiritual" pursuits). But is this assessment really justified? At first glance, it might seem so in the minds of those anxious to find fault with him (although one can't help but wonder how such an indictment would raise objection in the intensely commercial world of Venice). Shylock constantly speaks of little other than his business prospects or those of his competitors, and if such single-mindedness is a "crime" then he is surely guilty. But a compelling alternative was suggested to me from an unexpected source.

Years ago, a classmate of mine at *The London Academy of Music and Dramatic Art (LAMDA)* – a young woman with quintessentially WASP credentials – offered the observation that Shylock wasn't exclusively concerned with business affairs at all, but rather employed the vocabulary of business as the medium through which he related to the world around him. Moreover, she asserted, she had known many non-Jewish businesspeople who did the same! My friend further observed that oft-times in the face of tragedy and loss, grief is hidden behind a façade, a preoccupation with the mundane or matters of business.

To my mind, these were profound observations, which placed a rather vulgar scene (3.1) in which Shylock vacillates callously (if not idiotically) between bemoaning the loss of his daughter and the loss of his diamonds, in a wholly different light. As often interpreted, the scene is used to reinforce the image of Shylock as a materialistic and insensitive wretch, devoid of even rudimentary human sympathies, obsessed only with the loss of his money.

But what if we more charitably consider that Shylock is, however subliminally, mourning the loss of his daughter all the while; referring obliquely in confusion and grief to her as his "diamond", while trying desperately, from behind the emotional façade mentioned, to deal with the magnitude of his real loss – that of his child – in the only language he knows![42]

Such a reaction; complex, seemingly contradictory, confused, and confusing to the outside observer, is not out of character for a Jewish father pushed past his limits, and if we allow for such subtext, doesn't Shylock become a hugely more interesting and human character than the one-dimensional object of derision the alternative suggests? But here again, the possibility for a humanised Shylock is lost on those all too conditioned to think the worst of "the Jew".

A Mixed (Up) Marriage

I once overheard a discussion between two actors of my acquaintance that illustrates the problem of understanding *MV* in an historical context rather well. One was a lapsed Catholic, the other a practicing one (in a rather contemporary manner, or so I gathered), and they were discussing some "issues" the "lapsed" party was having with her companion, a Jewish man. She, the lapsed party, expressed some desire to rejoin the Church but complained that her "other half" simply could not abide being present there.

She described with some exasperation her partner's Woody Allen-like paranoia at attending Mass *("'They're all watching me!', he exclaimed...")* To which her interlocutor replied with yet greater exasperation and apparent incredulity, "My God, don't they know that *Jesus* was Jewish?!"

Don't they know, indeed! Now that the Church has finally figured it out, two thousand years of antisemitism goes down the memory hole without a trace! So much so, that even intelligent and otherwise worldly individuals like these actors just can't figure these Jews out! As if Catholicism is just another kind of Judaism or vice versa. So, what's the big deal? Let's be sure we really understand what was understood in Elizabethan times, in Elizabethan terms, and let the chips fall where they may.

Revelations of a "Union Maid"

The pursuit of a character may draw upon unusual and unexpected sources, all part of one's life experience. One such instance still prominent in my memory occurred in the Holy Land on the kibbutz where I was resident for three years, Kibbutz Beit Zera in the Jordan Valley. Periodically, groups of volunteers from abroad would arrive to spend a period of time working in the collective. They ran the gamut from young Zionists interested in kibbutz life, to American Jewish kids interested only in a very safe taste of life in Israel for a very limited period, to social democratic youth from Europe curious about the efficacy of socialism Israeli style, to a variety of young holidaymakers looking for cheap digs as they bummed around the Middle East.

On this occasion, I made the acquaintance of a pleasant but retiring young woman from the English Midlands (not Jewish) who was about to enter university on her return home. She struck me as intelligent, educated, and reasonably middle-class. The main thing about her that sticks in my memory was a sudden burst of pique at one of the other Brits among the volunteers whom she described acrimoniously (or at least as acrimoniously as her understated personality would allow) as "the sort who would have driven the buses during the General Strike".

Coming from a socialist background, I was immediately intrigued by this clear and unexpected expression of class hostility towards her compatriot. I inquired of her what she meant by this apparent epithet.

She explained that in 1926, during a crucial period for developing British trade-unionism, the fledgling movement called a nine-day General Strike which among other things shut down all British transport. This was seen at the time as a vital gamble on the solidarity of British workers and the impact of working-class institutions on the sympathies of the British public. In response, middle and upper-class Britons were aghast and vehemently hostile. And upper-class youth took it upon themselves as a "public service" (more accurately as a passive-aggressive "lark") to drive the buses themselves. By this sign of contempt for the workers they also hoped to break the strike.

Her revelation was extremely interesting to me for several reasons. First, let's remember she was talking about an incident of her father's generation (I gathered he had been involved in the union movement of that period) but she had clearly personalised his experience emotionally to the point that she related the story as if it had been her own.

Second, the incident was symbolic of a larger set of social relationships and antagonisms that in her mind had clearly not been resolved. So much so, that she made rather vehement assumptions about others based on these preconceptions, despite her rather unaggressive personality and lack of overwhelming evidence.

One might ask, if an otherwise normal young Englishwoman could harbour such intense animosities based upon long-standing grievances of her working-class family, how much more intense and obsessive might be the reservoir of grievance of Shylock and kin?

A Drama School Faux Pas

One unguarded comment is worth a world of explanation. Such was the case when a teacher of mine at drama school, who fancied herself rather "posh" and identified a little too readily with the "upper crust", thought she would put in context for us a reference to "the Jews" in Noel Coward's satire on the English "idle classes", *The Stately Homes of England:*

> *Our homes command extensive views.*
> *And with assistance from the Jews,*
> *we have been able to dispose of*
> *rows and rows and rows of*
> *Gainsboroughs and Lawrences...*

She was no doubt trying to show "good form", earnestly explaining that had it not been for "the Jews", many of England's treasured paintings might have gone abroad (probably to America, perish the thought)!

But consider for a moment the implications of her apologia (which really wasn't necessary in any event, since Coward's reference is transparently benign, taking the "mickey" out of upper-class *Brits*, not Jews).

After all, who were these "Jews"?

Whether a Rothschild or a similarly well-established Anglo-Jewish collector or philanthropist, the "Jews" in question, who on so many occasions, Coward suggests, secured the legacy of Britain for the British, were hardly newcomers (well maybe in comparison to the Celts they were, but come on!). Yet in the minds of many – the instructor in question apparently being one – they still didn't quite qualify as British.

And at what point do they become British?

Answer: not yet anyway, and probably never!

Quod Erat Demonstrandum!

When the Quality of Mercy is Strained, Indeed!

My comments on Portia's questionable virtues have a personal dimension to them which, while initially distressing, has with the passage of time taken on a certain humour because of its utter absurdity. It is a painful example of the wrath awaiting the apostate who dares to question the virtues of a hallowed saint of Shakespeare's canon. It is also an example of tunnel vision wrapped in a mantle of indignation that can make the world of Shakespeare-worship, its gatekeepers and "aficionados", theatrically stultifying.

I am referring to a discussion I once had with a former friend about this very subject of unconventional perspectives on Shakespeare and the characters in *MV*.

The friend was a successful Hollywood figure who took a keen interest in acting technique. We had a very friendly association for some time in an acting studio in L.A., and I naively entered a discussion with him on various aspects of my book, having done so on many other topics, with emphasis on what I saw as the grave shortcomings of the Venetian characters, including the much-vaunted, Portia.

In my zeal to make my point and thinking myself "among friends", I referred to Portia in the trial scene, rather provocatively with tongue-in-cheek, in less than "gentlemanly terms", given her unrelenting destruction of Shylock after her "Sermon on the Mount" on the "quality of mercy." Indeed, I said she seemed to me a version of the fictional Southern Belle who could wax romantic on the one hand, while malevolently turning upon her slaves as the spirit moved her, on the other.

This, to my shock, elicited from him a response of such vituperation that it appeared I had offended the man personally! What followed was a roasting of the most intense kind, ending with the reprimand that I should be "ashamed!" – when a simple objection, however impassioned, might have sufficed!

I never heard from him again.

I should have thought that after many years of cordial and productive association a slightly more "merciful" response from a champion of Portia would have been in order! But there it is!

The theatre is a dangerous place!

What Comes by Chance - A Shylock Found

Imagery useful to a production can come unexpectedly from many quarters. One Friday evening while driving home through a Jewish neighbourhood in Los Angeles, my eye caught sight of a solitary figure walking down the street, likely from a local synagogue. He appeared to be a middle-aged man of Middle Eastern origin dressed in a dark suit consistent with him coming from prayer (I assumed he was Mizrahi by his appearance and by there being many Iranian Jews in the neighbourhood).

What struck me about him quite vividly were a number of subtle distinctions and contradictions. Unlike others who passed that evening he was alone without family to accompany him, walking deliberately with a solitary and subdued air. To my eye he appeared past his prime, beginning to be slightly bowed by the adversities of advancing age and life and a bit "rough 'round the edges". But he nonetheless evinced the darkly handsome image of a man once vital in a lost youth.

For some reason, this man's sudden appearance and the aura surrounding him resonated deeply within me. I didn't know the man personally or anything about him but the sight of him reflexively awakened in my thoughts a backstory of loneliness, loss, and perseverance which moved me with the force I had experienced in the dream-state fantasies described in the preceding chapter. A moment unanticipated, spontaneous and emotionally stimulating for acting purposes, whether true in fact or not.

The thought suddenly flashed in my mind before I could articulate it in words:

This is my Shylock!

Stranger in a Strange Land

> We have sincerely tried everywhere to merge with the national communities in which we live, seeking only to preserve the faith of our fathers. It is not permitted us. In vain are we loyal patriots, sometimes superloyal; in vain do we make the same sacrifices of life and property as our fellow citizens; in vain do we strive to enhance the fame of our native lands in the arts and sciences, or her wealth by trade and commerce. In our native lands where we have lived for centuries we are still decried as aliens, often by men whose ancestors had not yet come at a time when Jewish sighs had long been heard in the country…
> *Theodore Herzl, founder of modern Zionism*

On September 15, 1935, with the passage of the Nuremberg Laws, over 500,000 German Jews, and other German citizens of "questionable" racial backgrounds by Nazi standards, suddenly became "foreigners" in their own country. Many so defined by the Nazi state had never thought of themselves as other than "German." Many knew nothing of their non-Aryan background, and their exclusion, both racist and arbitrary, was often without internal consistency even by perverted Nazi standards.

Thus, the status of an individual in Nazi Germany became hugely variable and uncertain, dependent upon the prejudices of the powers that be and the culture at large – the victims having nothing to say in the matter. Such a dynamic did not require the advent and extremes of Nazi racism, however; it had long been evidenced to lesser extremes since the rise of the European state system in which Jews were often defined as "alien", irrespective of how long they had lived in a particular society. In the most absurd of ironies, this was often the case in settings where Jewish communities dating back to Roman times had long predated the arrival of the "barbarians" who came be the very national majorities who defined them as foreign![43]

According to John Gross in *Shylock: A Legend and Its Legacy*, the Jewish community of Venice was divided into three subgroups:

> the 'German Nation', the 'Levantine Nation' and the 'Ponentine Nation' or 'Western Nation' made up of Spanish Jews and Marranos ... the 'Germans' were the only group in the ghetto permitted to practice money lending.[44]

But the members of each of these communities may well have been resident in Venice for many generations and need not have been distinguishable as foreign speakers.

Therefore, the fact that Shylock is perceived as "foreign" in the eyes of the Christians and designated so by the Venetian court, doesn't mean that he literally is so. As previously mentioned, highly assimilated German Jews, often of high culture, became "foreigners" overnight in Nazi Germany and the questions surrounding Shylock's status in Christian society becomes even more poignant if he is "foreign" only in the minds of his xenophobic detractors – adding an additional layer of "insult to injury" with which he must contend (and a cruel irony which Shakespeare himself may have intended). This possibility may have been suggested by Shakespeare in the trial scene (4.1) when Portia, in her guise as a Doctor of Laws come to defend Antonio, asks the curious question, "Which is the merchant here and which the Jew?"

The implications of this question raise several intriguing possibilities. It may be that the query is simply an element of her disguise confirming before the court her status as a foreign counsel unfamiliar with the parties to the case. It may reflect her actual social distance and that of Belmont from both Antonio and Shylock, truly suggesting her unfamiliarity with both men. Or, more interestingly, Shakespeare may be suggesting here that there really isn't much to distinguish plaintiff and defendant socially or ethnically, thereby heightening the irrationality of the conflict between them.

A production with Laurence Olivier as Shylock essentially did this, with Shylock being largely indistinguishable in dress and social status from the Venetians around him. Such an assumption, moreover, would be altogether consistent with the long history of Jewish residence in Venice which for certain segments of the population, as mentioned above, extended back to Roman times. Thus, some interesting options arise regarding Shylock's cultural background and his status vis à vis the Christian society around him and how the character might be portrayed in performance.

CONCEPT AND SETTING
The Mandate Connection: A Political Odyssey

My choice of setting *MV* in British Mandatory Palestine in the immediate post-war period is one of personal significance to me, in addition to serving what I hope will be an innovative dramatic purpose. It reflects, moreover, an ideological crisis affecting my thinking about the drama, the interpretation of the character, Shylock, and my own political perspectives, as I will demonstrate.

I came from a Labour-Zionist family and for a time thoroughly identified with the concept of the "New Jew" conceived by that ideology – that unique creation born of Jewish Nationalism, Jewish Socialism, and the sun, air, and Land of Israel. This new departure in Jewish history (and, by implication, world history) was to embody the accumulated acuity, genius, and moral sensibilities of diaspora Jewish culture with the fortitude, muscularity, and heroic Spartacism of a generation born in and close to the "Land of our Fathers" ("Eretz Avoteinu").

Within the Zionist movement itself, the rift between the traditional image of the Jew and this Jewish "Brave New World" played out in often deep-seated animosities between Labour-Zionists and Zionist Revisionists. The former was led by the socialist, David Ben-Gurion and the kibbutz movement that dominated the quasi-governmental

Jewish Agency for Palestine; the latter by Vladimir (Ze'ev) Jabotinsky and, after WWII, by Menachem Begin who led a militant but small minority faction of the Yishuv (the Jewish community of Palestine) called the Irgun whose focus was more strictly nationalist without concern for social utopianism.

The Labour Zionists professed a commitment to restraint and cooperation with Britain to the extent possible. The Irgun and its even more extreme ally the Stern group believed, in contrast, that restraint in the face of British denial of Jewish immigration was to no avail; that the plight of Europe's Jews demanded a war of national liberation against British rule without inhibition, to open the gates of Palestine to the survivors of Hitler's carnage. They declared all-out war on Britain with the kind of violence seen in other uprisings throughout its empire.

It would be safe to say that the lodestar of our ideology was the reflexive dismissal of Menachem Begin as a "Fascist". So, it came as something of a shock to me – in fact, a source of outright cognitive dissonance – when I discovered later in life that this accusation was simply not true. Not even a matter of interpretation, it was a bald-faced lie and a libel all too glibly indulged in by leftists against anyone who didn't meet with their ideological approval – including, at times, other leftists.

Now, I say this without endorsing Mr. Begin's ideology in all its aspects, nor turning a blind eye to excesses that were committed by some of his followers. But the following discoveries led me to a thoroughgoing reassessment of political "truths" long-held uncritically. Namely, that he originally came out of a leftist background himself – the Socialist-Zionist, Hashomer Hatzair (The Young Guard) youth movement in Poland[45] – before becoming a supporter of Jabotinsky's Zionist Revisionist movement; that as a mature politician, he never espoused any sympathy for totalitarian systems of the right or the left;

and that as prime minister he scrupulously honoured the rights of his parliamentary opponents however vociferous their animosity towards him. (I have testimony to this effect from a prominent left-wing Knesset [Parliament] member in Israel, who told me that Begin treated him impeccably while he was afforded no similar courtesies by Labour Party opponents).[46]

In a real sense, the denigration of Begin, it seemed to me, was a modern incarnation of the vilification of Shylock, and I don't say that pejoratively regarding either of them. They both were men grievously wronged,[47] who responded to persecution as men are wont to do in the Christian world (i.e., violently), not as "Jews" bent on self-deprecation, ideological purity, or sainthood. Were they Irish, they would have been lionised in story and song, but as Jews they are denied that privilege, even by their own people.

Indeed, Begin and Shylock are despised for much the same reason. Not because they hate without cause and not because they resort to tactics unprecedentedly vindictive. When you stop to think about the panorama of wars, inquisitions, gas chambers, and bloodlettings so central to the European experience, "a pound of flesh" is rather modest by Christian standards![48] And Shakespeare's canon itself is replete with child murder, eye-gouging, mutilation, cannibalism, and other deadly mayhem, apparently accepted by his audiences as "standard operating procedure" in the culture of its day. Especially unfair are the calumnies directed against Menachem Begin who, far from demanding "a pound of flesh" from his adversaries – even in the context of a revolutionary and existential conflict – imposed upon his followers standards of selectivity in the use of violence that compared altogether favourably or surpassed those of other national liberation movements, ranging from the IRA and ANC to the American revolutionists.

No. The violence acceptable in others, even lauded in the bronzed, statuesque Spartans of the Socialist-Zionist underground fighters,

Haganah and its elite strike force the Palmach, is reviled in the visage of the homely, gap-toothed, bespectacled, Levantine, ghetto Jew that, in the minds of many – especially in the jaundiced view of his British adversaries – Begin epitomised. This double standard is hypocritical, dehumanising, morally vacuous, and cruel, and is rooted both in the symbiotic relationship of Christian Jew hatred and disparagement, and in its progeny: Jewish self-hatred, and self-deprecation.

My choice of setting offers the added attraction, dramatically and historically, of an anti-British resistance movement, the aforementioned "Irgun", led by Mr. Begin, which in the eyes of the British had many of the qualities of parochial extremism and stereotype that they associated with the traditional Shylock himself. Thus, British authorities of the period can be placed effectively in parallel with their bigoted Venetian counterparts in the play and, unfortunately, there is much in the records of British officialdom in Palestine and the Foreign Office to make that relationship concrete.

I don't see Shylock initially driven by ideology. In my conception, he starts out a very apolitical man preoccupied with mundane matters of business and family affairs. But in the course of the play, due to the mounting indignities of Christian hate, and broken by the loss of his daughter and his forced conversion to Christianity, Shylock finds himself at the Irgun's door. It is this breakdown and conversion of a common man to an extremist and his tortuous path in getting there which is most interesting, in my view, and adds a vital dimension of reality to the character of Shylock in modern terms. Thus, his excesses are brought into the well-known and believable realm of anti-imperialist struggle and retribution, providing a timely dimension to the play's interpretation on a road well-travelled vis à vis Britain: from the Americans to the Irish, to the Indians, to the Jews of Palestine and beyond.

And so, in establishing a historical and dramatic bridge between the excesses of Shylock and the putative extremism of the Irgun, we see the ancient agonies of oppressed Jewry embodied in a modern Jewish resistance movement of the post-Holocaust world: a movement born of the despair of a downtrodden people; a last remnant of hope for victims of a world denuded of mercy and dashed beyond recognition or recovery; a revolt shorn of illusions and moderation grasping salvation for tortured humanity through violent struggle, sacrifice, and blood; the last hope for many who have suffered a full measure of the world's scorn and fallen hopelessly beyond its pity.

The struggle to free Mandatory Palestine from the yoke of British domination and to open its gates to the surviving remnant of their brethren – no matter the cost – was seen by the Irgun and its supporters as their raison d'être; their fevered demand for justice in the face of an uncaring world, à la Shylock before the Venetian tribunal; and their last defence and bulwark against utter desolation, both personal and collective.

In the proposed setting, characters representing the Irgun underground clandestinely bear witness to Shylock's torment as a silent chorus that weaves through the play, emerging just before the final curtain as the agents of his redemption when defeat seems most complete and loss irredeemable.

Note:
For those who may reflexively take offence or be overly pleased by the mention of Menachem Begin and Shylock in the same breath, I must reiterate the quote by the great Hollywood screenwriter and journalist, Ben Hecht, in the Introduction to this work:

I have felt sorry that so many Jews ... fail to recognize Shylock as their brother and turn their backs on him. I have never found Shylock to be the villain against whom Jews keep protesting as a libel of their kind. To the contrary, he is one of the few heroic Jews in classic literature, perhaps even the only one.

Ben Hecht was a great partisan of Menachem Begin and the Irgun (as was the acclaimed actor and acting teacher Stella Adler. My purpose here is to demonstrate that contrary to the beliefs of some, neither Shylock nor Begin (whose mother, father, and brother were brutally murdered at the hands of the Nazis, as were most of the community from which he came should be viewed as villains, but rather as representatives of the extremes to which even decent people may go in the face of oppression and in reaction to the injustices they have suffered.

Thus, sympathisers need not grieve, and detractors should not gloat.

As the curtain falls, we realise that Shylock's existence now has a larger revolutionary purpose that had previously eluded him. That in resistance, his suffering, and the impulse to violence that it generates, will find a new, disciplined direction and meaning, and that his passion will not go unanswered.

In the process, we see the character of Shylock dramatically transformed and our image of him and the meaning of MV is transformed as well.

Struck, Hermann: Russian Jew from Odessa *(detail)*
Leo Baeck Institute, 81.385.

PART TWO

The Merchant of Venice (MV), as adapted here,
is the story of a 'common man' driven to uncommon extremes:
the tale of a broken man impelled by cruelty and degradation
to vengeance beyond his imagining …
And the story of those who drove him there.

Image credit: kuan@watersedge, Flickr

ADAPTATION AND TREATMENT

The Story

MV provides a dramatic vehicle for reflection on the crimes at the heart of Western civilisation – in particular the persecution of the Jews – even as it deals forthrightly with the ancillary question of extremes; the lengths to which victims of oppression may go in seeking retribution for their abuse. And this, it seems to me, is a dimension of our history that must be confronted morally and has much to say, dramatically, about the state of our world today.

* * *

MV as adapted here is the story of a "common man" driven to uncommon extremes. It is the story of Shylock, a Jew beset at every turn – "'buked and scorned", in the words of the old spiritual – cheated of dignity by bigotry and circumstance, pushed to the edge of madness by a violence foreign to his character and people.

Our narrative explores the psychology of a broken man, and the cruelties and degradations that can drive by corrosive increments the most unassuming of men to an unimaginable ferocity. It explores the limits of forbearance on a personal level in a setting that tests the forbearance of a people on a national level: post-war Mandatory Palestine and the conflict between Britain and the Jews that ensued there.

For our purposes, modern British imperialism, and ruling-class antisemitism, reflecting religious and social prejudices of long standing, take the place of the bigotries of Shakespeare's Venice. And the abuse suffered by "the Jew" Shylock on a personal level, is mirrored in the larger travails and struggles of the Jewish People on a national level and their struggle for safe-haven and survival in Palestine in the face of Nazi brutality and British insensitivity and contempt.

In pursuing this end, two traditional approaches to the interpretation of *MV* are rejected outright: first, and most emphatically, the antisemitic tradition of "Shylock-as-Villain", fiendish grotesque, the embodiment of inveterate "Jewish evil" – a view widely held, uncritically, in Shakespeare's day and repeated in various forms for centuries thereafter; and, second, the romanticised reaction to that tradition, "Shylock-as-Martyr", with its implications of exoticism and hapless ineffectuality. Both these perspectives, in my view, reduce Shylock to the level of eccentricity and stereotype, robbing him of the full complexity and humanity to which a modern audience can relate.

Our Shylock doesn't fit the historical mould, socially, psychologically, or aesthetically. He is not the easily recognisable parochial stereotype of Eastern Europe so often applied to the part despite its Venetian setting, nor is he an inherently hateful person. He is, rather, for our purposes, a Sephardic Jew of Greek origin, richly endowed with the culture of an ancient community and a backstory of personal tragedy that precedes and accentuates his travails of the text.

Shylock is a man deeply moved by memories of his late wife, Leah, which we know from a revealing interchange with Tubal (3.1) when, in a moment of weakness and rage, he laments the loss of his "turquoise", a ring given him by Leah when he was a bachelor, at the profligate hands of his estranged daughter, Jessica. His sudden deep remorse at the loss of this intimate keepsake suggests a degree of sentiment and vulnerability that humanises our perception of him and illuminates his conflicted and painful state of mind.

Our narrative will propose that Shylock's beloved wife, Leah, has died of cancer at the beginning of the War (an element that will be established visually through a dream-dance sequence similar in kind to the death scene in the ballet, *La Dame aux Camélias* by John Neumeier, created for Marcia Haydée of the *Stuttgart Ballet*), leaving him a bereft widower with a young daughter, Jessica. But he is cruelly forced to sublimate his grief and leave his mourning unresolved by the immediate threat of Nazi invasion in 1941, forcing his desperate flight literally from Leah's graveside to Jewish Palestine (the Yishuv) with his little daughter.

Shylock's deep loss, emotionally unresolved, is an unspoken dimension of his character as we later find him colouring his interaction with the world as he struggles to reconstruct his life in Jerusalem. Over the years, he establishes himself successfully in business, his struggle for existence and that of his daughter his sole preoccupation, the battle with his demons his narrow obsession. He is a lonely man, unconnected to the dynamic society evolving around him, its social norms, and ideologies. He walks separately and alone, carrying with him painful remembrance of his former life while negotiating each day his soul's emptiness.

Affairs of business appear to be Shylock's overwhelming, outward concern; the prism through which he views the world and the vocabulary by which he communicates with it. He is not devoid of sentiment but is inadequate to the task of expressing it – a deficit easily misunderstood by all and exploited by his detractors. He has no clear path in life, save putting one foot in front of the other, day by day, assessing existence by prosaic measures of profit and loss, and resisting all that would threaten his rigidly imposed equilibrium. He is not of his place and time, nor possessed of a vision beyond it. He is a coil ever more tightly wound.

If these personal adversities were Shylock's only concerns, they would be burden enough, but he inevitably finds himself entwined in the larger tapestry of tragedy and turmoil roiling the world into which he has been cast. Despite his best efforts to remain aloof from the life around him, the defensive walls of Shylock's private world are increasingly breached by the traumas unfolding before him.

In the course of the play, Shylock bears witness, despite his will, to acts of violent repression by British authorities and their moral insensitivity to the hapless refugees on their shores. These affronts to humanity, which he can no longer ignore, awaken in him a long-dormant sense of connection to the suffering of others and a growing outrage at the personal indignities to which he has long been subjected. The opening of his consciousness to this larger world of suffering sets the stage for his transformation, in the wake of his ultimate humiliation at the hands of his Christian tormentors of forced conversion, from an isolated and hapless victim to an active resister taking his fate and dignity into his own hands.

This painful odyssey of liberation rising from the ashes of defeat is at the heart of the following interpretation and treatment of Shylock's story and the play's conflict. This transformation is a motif essential to my conception of the play and the resolution of its plot in a manner designed to render Shylock fully human in the manner of aggrieved resisters of other lands.

Understanding Shylock's struggle further requires insight into the prejudices of his adversaries and the abuses to which they are prone.

The British, motivated by realpolitik and social prejudice, have capitulated to Arab demands to deny Europe's Jews haven in Palestine

– the homeland long promised them by Britain. Jewish rage at the complicity of British policies in the monstrous devastation of the Holocaust has incited violent rebellion. Two resistance organisations – the *Irgun Zvai Leumi* (the National Military Organisation) and the *Stern Group* (*Gang*, in the minds of some), moved to militancy by revolutionary creed and calamitous personal losses of the Holocaust, are no longer willing to abide by policies of "self-restraint" ("havlagah" in Hebrew) in dealings with Britain, the hallmark of the majority-supported Jewish Agency and its defence organisations, *Haganah* (The Defence) and its elite *Palmach* (Strike-force). They now embark upon an unrestrained assault against the British occupation and its restrictions on Jewish immigration. Irgun and Sternist violence begins to take a devastating toll on British forces, and the colonial administration, a class often prone to less than complimentary sentiments towards Jews at the best of times, responds with increasing repression.

In this, we see a provocative parallel between the mindset of prominent British officials in Mandatory Palestine and the prejudices of Christian Venice embodied in *MV*'s main characters: Antonio, Gratiano, the servant Launcelot Gobbo and perhaps most disturbingly in the refined condescension and self-importance of the much-vaunted Portia. In both contexts, high-minded "Christian virtues" are belied by actual Christian behaviour – a crucial dimension of the play's conflict – and the Venetians of the original setting are found appropriate corollaries in British Mandatory society.

This atmosphere of contempt for "the Jew(s)" is a corrosive element of Shylock's daily existence, which, in the wake of unrelenting affronts and the devastating loss of his daughter to the world of Christian decadence, pushes him beyond the limits of rationality – of sanity even. His aberrant and obsessive demand for a promised "pound of flesh" from his nemesis, Antonio, as collateral for his forfeited loan, reflects the rage and disorientation that afflict him. His demand for Antonio's flesh, whether arguable or not as a matter of Venetian law, is so far removed from civilised norms (and Jewish law) as to be deemed abhorrent and proves his undoing.

In a more rational mind, the futility of such vengeance and the probability of its defeat would be clear; but Shylock, driven to near madness by grief, personal loss, and resentment, is consumed by the desire for revenge and unable to anticipate the trap that awaits him. His ill-considered obsession for blood retribution, in a manner it must be emphasised that is totally anathema to Jewish values (a measure, in this interpretation, which he shrinks from even as he is about to exact the penalty at trial), is thoroughly defeated by the court, leaving him open to counterattack and reprisal at the hands of an antisemitic establishment. The resulting court-imposed conversion of "the Jew" to Christianity makes his defeat and abasement altogether complete.

(It must be noted that forced conversion would not have been a true option in British Palestine, but this is a dramatic problem that plagues all efforts at modernised settings of the play and must be accepted as a convention if the text is to be strictly followed. This problem could be addressed by simply ignoring the anomaly, portraying the court as acting corruptly beyond all proper standards of modern colonial administration, or by momentarily suspending parameters of time and place to allow the court to function in style and dress as if it were returned to Elizabethan times, etc.)

As these travails play out, privileged segments of British/Venetian society, embodied in idyllic Belmont, pursue lives of grand oblivion to the tragedies and injustices unfolding on their doorstep. Their licentious abandon as revealed by a grand and raucous soirée hosted by Portia dramatises this dichotomy and heightens the perversity of their prejudice and general disregard for the inferior "colonials" in their world of empire.

In this cauldron of conflicting worlds, we see a kaleidoscope of battling subtexts and interests as a backdrop to the main action of the play, providing new context and colour to its interpretation and meaning. These include images of the daily life and diversity of the Yishuv (Jewish community of Palestine); its internal frictions and interactions with British occupation forces; the ominous presence of rump-Nazi operatives and Mosleyite pro-fascist collaborators aiding Arab insurgents in a continuing war against the Jews of Palestine even after the German defeat in Europe; and the clandestine Jewish resistance driven on occasion to extremes, à la Shylock himself, in the face of these retrograde adversaries.

As mentioned before, an intriguing subtext will also be seen in the unexpected presence of a coterie of young Irgun operatives observably moving in and out of scenes in a variety of guises – noting, assessing, and, at the end of the play, intervening to resurrect Shylock in the wake of his devastation at the hands of the Mandatory courts and the perfidy of his daughter. Through their intercession at his nadir, he is delivered from ruin and given haven and salvation in the world of resistance which now provides meaning and purpose to his suffering – his remonstrance to Antonio, his oath and call to arms: *"The villainy you teach me I will execute - and it shall go hard but I will better the instruction!"* (3.1).

His oath a prelude to an explosive ending…

***

Thus, we see a drama played out of universal import: the agony of the "common man" – apolitical, bereft of hope, a maddened victim of forces beyond his control. The transformation of his consciousness from extremes of submission or irrational violence to disciplined revolt against his fate and tormentors and the rising of the masses against tyranny and oppression – a story oft-repeated in the affairs of subject peoples and colonial powers of our age.

By virtue of these interpretive elements a new Shylock emerges, recognisable in modern psychological and political terms. A man whose behaviour, however extreme, is not without cause and of a kind with liberation struggles, resistance movements, and revolutions common to the 20th century often marked by excesses of their own.

Thus, a fully human and dramatic story is revealed consistent with modern understanding, separating *MV* from an unworthy tradition of ghoulish fantasy, racial bigotry, and degrading stereotype too long associated with the play and its signature character, Shylock, the Jew.

How this will be done, our Treatment now will show.

THE MERCHANT OF VENICE
Based on the Play by William Shakespeare

Story by Alan Bergreen

Copyright © Alan Bergreen 2017.

All rights reserved.

WGA Registration 2017

DRAMATIS PERSONAE

ANTONIO, a military attaché to the diplomatic corps in Palestine.

SALARIO, a north-country non-com of playful demeanour. One half of the Salario-Solanio comedy double act.

SOLANIO, The other half of the comic duo.

BASSANIO, a young, handsome man of upper-class bearing, a captain in the British forces in Palestine, and a distant relation of Antonio, though something in their rapport seems beyond a mere familial affection.

LORENZO, a young lieutenant, Bassanio's junior in rank and age, with an air of naïve decency about him that sets him apart from the upper-class demeanour of his colleagues.

GRATIANO, a mid-level CID officer noted for his heavy-handed tactics. A social climbing thug, sexual chauvinist, and closet Mosleyite (Fascist sympathiser), he adopts a veneer of respectability and bonhomie only to the extent it serves him. But his true colours, his coarseness, and his antisemitism are ever-near the surface, crudely expressed towards Shylock and further manifested in his shady dealings with Arab extremists and Nazi operatives still active in Palestine on behalf of the Grand Mufti. Gratiano, as certain of his ilk will do, eventually deserts British forces and offers his services to Fawzi al-Kawukji's Arab Liberation Army in attacks upon the nascent State of Israel.

SHYLOCK, a Sephardic Jew, of Greek origin, who has suffered the grievous loss of his wife during the war, barely escaping to Palestine ahead of the Nazi invasion of Salonika with his young daughter Jessica.

JESSICA, Shylock's daughter, coming of age and smitten with love for Lorenzo; rebellious and resentful of the limitations placed upon her by a domineering father and her minority social status.

LAUNCELET GOBBO, Shylock's wayward Arab shop assistant and gadfly, ever eager to provoke his boss and lend a sympathetic ear to Jessica's complaints.

PORTIA, daughter of a high-ranking British military man and love interest of Bassanio. A modern woman and feminist, she feels with intensity the injustice of the constraints placed upon her by family obligations and position, especially as regards her choice of husband – a disposition which makes her "fall" for Bassanio the more dramatic and amusing. Her "modernity" and other enchanting qualities, however, do not translate into more favourable attitudes toward Jews (or people of colour) than others of her class, infusing her "high-minded" admonitions to Shylock at trial and her initial faux-liberality towards the Prince of Morocco with a haughty air of hypocrisy.

NERISSA, Portia's working-class lady-in-waiting and confidante. A perceptive woman of active intelligence, Nerissa aspires to the modern fashions of her mistress, but remains the more grounded of the two due to her working-class origins.

OLD GOBBO, Launcelet's father.

THE GENERAL, Shakespeare's Duke, who for our purposes will either be a distinguished looking, greying British Governor of Palestine with a benevolent exterior cloaking a distaste for the Jews, or a sharp-featured weasel of a man with a malevolent charm.

Suitors for Portia's hand of various national backgrounds.
Supporting roles, incl. military tribunal members, Arab and Jewish men and women in the street, British soldiers, Irgun operatives, jazz musicians, socialites, and other extras as deemed necessary.

Makram J. Khoury plays Shylock in an RSC 2015 production, *Dir: Polly Findlay*.
Image used with the permission of the RSC.

PRELUDE

British Mandatory Palestine, 1946

The audience assembles to a montage projected on screens of sights and sounds of British Mandatory Palestine: newsreel footage of British forces under Gen. Allenby entering triumphantly into Jerusalem in WWI; Zionist pioneers reclaiming the land; Arab life in cities and rural villages; the rise of Bauhaus Tel Aviv; followed by the rise of Nazism in Germany, WWII and destruction of Europe's Jews; with images of Jewish survivors in desperate search of refuge and British efforts to bar their entry to Palestine.

These images are punctuated by music, speeches, and sounds of life fleshing out the history and environment of Palestine in the post-war period when the play is set. As the montage progresses, images dramatically juxtaposing the life of the Jewish populace and that of their British High Church overlords gain increasing prominence. When the house is full, the montage builds to a crescendo, then goes black and silent.

After several beats, lights slowly go up, revealing:

A street in Jerusalem's Old City adjacent to the Jaffa Gate.

Dead of night. Resounding silence, punctuated by sounds of the odd night-bird or cat amplified by stone walls and streets.

A single streetlamp casts sharp shadows down the hard stones of streets and walls. A solitary light burns in a lifeless upper-floor window overlooking the scene. An expectant stillness prevails.

Suddenly, silence is broken. Muffled sounds of whispers and furtive feet on cobblestones approach the illuminated street.

Three clandestine figures - two darkly clad young men and a woman - emerge suddenly from the shadows and rapidly set about their evening's work plastering stone walls and shop windows with propaganda posters of the militant resistance movement "Irgun Zvai Leumi".

Their work is suddenly interrupted by the sound of an approaching vehicle, opening of car doors and rapid advance of heavy shoes and boots on the cobblestone street.

The group leader urgently signals his comrades to break off their efforts, dragging the young woman in his charge away from a poster half-plastered on the window of S. Lock & Co, Ltd. - Currency & Credit *which flaps limply on the pane.*

The three run rapidly down a darkened side street just as agents of the British CID (Criminal Investigations Department), with Arab deputies in tow, round the bend (led by a thuggish officer we will later come to know as Gratiano).

The CID pause momentarily, get their bearings, take in the offending posters and then, amidst muted curses, careen after the disappearing sounds of the three underground fighters.

Shouts and shots are heard in the distance. Then dead silence.

After a moment, a black cat emerges from its lair and rapidly crosses the street, mouse in jaws. The night-bird issues an agitated whistle and flutters from its perch. The lone light in the upstairs window suddenly goes dark, as does the scene.

ACT ONE

1.1

An officers' "social club", strewn with artifacts of a previous night's revelries and debaucheries.

Antonio, a military attaché to the diplomatic corps in Palestine, sits at a table, stage right, head in hands, staring morosely through a bay-window into the first rays of morning. He bemoans his state of melancholy, claiming to be at a loss to understand it or himself.

Salario, a north-country non-com of playful demeanour, is revealed by the spreading light strewn on a large sofa up-centre of Antonio. He stirs and awakens to find a pair of lady's undergarments partially obscuring his face which he removes with a start, groans, and takes up the tedious discourse with Antonio of the night before, rationalising his anxiety as a normal concern for his ships and cargoes at sea, nothing more.

Meanwhile, Solanio (also of provincial background), Salario's comedy-team "other half", has awakened at the sofa's other end with a female body in a state of dishabille wedged between him and the cushions. He raises the sheet partially covering his companion to reveal a naked derrière, which, to his amusement, he sharply and unceremoniously slaps, eliciting the indignant exit of his companion amid a flurry of bedsheets, dishevelled garments, and expletives in Arabic. His romantic ventures at an end, he abruptly joins, with feigned earnestness, the pressing discussion of Antonio's distress.

Salario and Solanio compete, in ever more elaborate justifications, to explain Antonio's unease, all premised on the anxieties attendant to his mercantile ventures. But Antonio rejects their ministrations, stating firmly, in effect, that "his eggs are not all in one basket", he doesn't fear the loss of his merchandise, and that can't be the reason he's so sad.

Solanio, probing facetiously, suggests that Antonio "must be in love". Antonio defensively dismisses the suggestion out of hand. But Solanio knows he's on to something and continues to elicit a reaction from him by way of satirically musing that some personalities will laugh too easily at the slightest provocation while others can't be made to smile no matter how good the joke is! Antonio's evasions provide foreshadowing of a secret yet to be learned about him and his emotions. But the tension is abruptly broken by the sudden entry of three comrades:

Enter BASSANIO, LORENZO, and GRATIANO.

Bassanio is a young, handsome man of upper-class bearing and a captain in the British forces in Palestine. He is a distant relation of Antonio, though there is something in their rapport that seems beyond mere familial affection (which may be the source of Antonio's unexplained melancholy as Bassanio's interests blossom in the direction of Portia).

His companion, Lorenzo, is a young lieutenant, Bassanio's junior in rank and age, with an air of naïve decency about him that sets him apart from the upper-class demeanour of his colleagues.

The third of the group, Gratiano, just back from his night duties as resistance hunter, is a mid-level CID officer noted for his heavy-handed tactics. A social climbing thug, sexual chauvinist, and closet Mosleyite (Fascist sympathiser), he adopts a veneer of respectability and bonhomie only to the extent it serves him. But his true colours, his coarseness, and his antisemitism are ever-near the surface, regularly expressed towards Shylock and further manifest in his shady dealings with Arab extremists and Nazi operatives still active in Palestine on behalf of Haj Amin el-Husseini, the Nazi allied Grand Mufti of Jerusalem. Gratiano, as certain of his ilk will do, eventually deserts the British forces, and offers his services to Fawzi al-Kawukji's Arab Liberation Army in its attack upon the nascent State of Israel.

Solanio hails the threesome, making a point, with thinly veiled humour, of Bassanio's arrival on the scene. He takes their arrival as cue to depart, with Salario, picking up his role in the comedy double-act, also announcing his exit. Antonio, now totally pre-occupied with the arrival of Bassanio, ignores their jibes and with feigned cordiality endorses their wish to depart.

Bassanio, unaware of the preceding interchange between Antonio and the two "clowns" and its subtext, is surprised by their sudden change of demeanour. He objects to their leaving and asks when they will rejoin the revelries. To which Salario, evasively playing the innocent, responds, in effect, "any time you like".

Lorenzo, taking in the scene, senses a need for privacy between Antonio and Bassanio. He also takes his leave, reminding Bassanio not to forget their meeting place later for dinner. Bassanio assures him he will not.

Gratiano, ever eager to ingratiate himself, picks up the discussion of Antonio's health and state of mind, declaring his feigned concern that Antonio is taking life too seriously. He warns him that this is the surest way to get hurt, that the ill-effects can already be seen in him, and that he looks not himself.

Antonio, effusing self-pity, responds to Gratiano (and through Gratiano to Bassanio nearby) that the world is just a stage upon which every person must act, and that he has been given a sad part to play (and there's nothing he can do about it).

Gratiano, in effort to appear wise as well as sympathetic, holds forth philosophically on the virtues of being merry. He disparages those who wish to appear wise by virtue of their reticence. He questions why any living man would wish to sit still like a statue and give himself ulcers by being constantly ill-humoured. And he couches his encouragement in professions of love for Antonio and the desire to see him well. But having fully played his hand he knows when to make his exit and draws Lorenzo with him, promising to resume his ministrations after dinner.

Lorenzo satirises Gratiano's grandiloquence, which, he quips in parting, has reduced him to the status of one of those silent "wise men" he ridiculed, unable to get a word in edge-wise. To which Gratiano, thoroughly full of himself and confident in his egotistical display, declares that if Lorenzo stays with him for two years he'll forget the sound of his own voice – for he'll never let him speak!

Antonio, eager to be rid of Gratiano, and recognising a windbag when he hears one, sends him off with the idle flattery that his lecture has miraculously brought his tongue to life.

Gratiano, in full sail, thanks him, and in a final show of vapid wit declares that the only tongues that should be silent are ox tongues for eating and those of old maids – upon which he and Lorenzo make their exits, leaving Antonio and Bassanio, finally, alone together.

Antonio and Bassanio are awkwardly silent together in a moment pregnant with subtext. They each have an agenda of which they find it hard to speak openly. Finally, Antonio breaks the ice obliquely by asking Bassanio if he thinks Gratiano's opinions are right. To which Bassanio, with equal evasion, replies that Gratiano is the biggest purveyor of nonsense in all of Venice whose arguments are a huge waste of time and whose point is meaningless.

A moment's further silence. Antonio gingerly approaches the matter on his mind. He hesitantly enquires about the lady in whom Bassanio has expressed interest and with whom he is planning a secret rendezvous. Feigning disinterest, he reminds Bassanio of his promise to relate the details.

Bassanio, suspects the jealousy at the root of Antonio's inquiry and parries his query by circuitously talking "business". He avoids

Antonio's subject head on by appealing to his sympathies regarding the bad state of his finances. Bassanio further disarms him by apologetically admitting his own profligacy and lifestyle beyond his means.

With studied humility, he declares that he knows he's been wrong and must exert greater personal discipline. Furthermore, he says, he's not complaining, he just wants to do the right thing, pay off his burgeoning debts to so many people, and acknowledges his great debt to Antonio to whom he owes the most in both money and love.

Since he knows Antonio loves him, too, he feels confident he can confide in him a plan he's hatched to get clear of all the debt he owes – an ingratiating and, in any case, unnecessary ploy since his assent is already assured.

Antonio is hooked. He rejects the need for further pleas telling Bassanio that trying to convince him further suggests he doesn't really believe in the sincerity of his love, a state to him worse than bankruptcy. He implores Bassanio to just tell him what he needs to do, and he will do it (hook, line, and sinker).

Bassanio now feels emboldened to relate his "plan"; a scheme which he knows Antonio must view, at best, with ambivalence, despite the mature and "sophisticated" nature of their relationship. But Bassanio has no shame when it suits his purposes.

He relates in vivid and glowing detail a description of a new-found love interest; a lady in Belmont named Portia, who is not only beautiful but virtuous, and, better still, fabulously wealthy by inheritance rivalling her namesake, Cato's daughter, and wife of Brutus of old. Her wealth is world famous, and there is an international competition underway to win her hand.

Bassanio is convinced that Portia has shown an interest in him. Confident in his psychological advantage, he brazenly wishes out loud to Antonio that if only he had enough money to "get in the game" he could win her (and then everyone gets paid off, old boy!)

Antonio is momentarily immobilised by the prospect of a real rival materialising before his eyes. He suddenly displays reticence towards Bassanio, reminding him that all his resources are tied up in his cargoes at sea and the cash on hand is not sufficient for his scheme. But just as quickly he realises the utility for his purposes of Bassanio's dependence upon his largesse. He "magnanimously" tells Bassanio to pursue his plan to get to Belmont and, "fair Portia", with whatever credit the two of them can muster about town, which Antonio feels sure he can secure as a business loan or personal favour. (Thus, their mutual exploitation proceeds).

Exeunt.

[1.1a – insert]

A square near the Jaffa Gate, Jerusalem

Lights come up again on the streets and square near the Jaffa Gate. Walls and storefronts reveal the militant propaganda campaign of the night before yet to be seen by the waking town. A lone Arab shopkeeper emerges from the store next to S. Lock & Co., stoically observes the poster marring his door, proceeds to remove it and then sets up a system of stalls with colourful trinkets and dry goods.

The street is slowly coming to life in the early morning light - an Arab boy laboriously pushes a cart laden with sesame-covered breads and hard pretzels into the square, an Armenian Orthodox Priest with long beard and flowing robes walks resolutely to church, two Catholic nuns almost collide with a pair of Chassidic youth late for prayer at the Western Wall in a jumble of seemingly identical black costumes (all parties with their minds on God rather than their temporal paths). A Mandatory policeman arrives on his morning rounds and calls in a report on the latest graffiti. Various and sundry workers, sightseers, and businesspeople, women with children in tow, and students on their way to school pass through the square in growing numbers.

Amid this growing and colourful mélange our eye is suddenly caught by a gaunt dark-clad figure emerging into sight from a side-street, (UL) uphill of the square. He proceeds methodically down the street feeding into the square out of step with the bustling life blossoming around him and largely oblivious to it, proceeding resolutely to his destination with eyes riveted on a newspaper well-folded into manageable sections with current stock prices that he meticulously examines and documents with a small stub of pencil.

Upon reaching the square he reflexively turns right on the way to his shop a few doors down and is suddenly greeted by his Arab neighbour. The two men have long known each other and have cordial relations. They embrace in the Eastern manner that is common to them both. But, almost in the same motion, Shylock's neighbour turns away, directing his attention to the defaced storefront of his shop.

Suddenly, Shylock's preoccupied demeanour alights with a flash of anger. He moves swiftly to his shop to examine the damage, at which point his wayward Arab shop assistant, Launcelet Gobbo, appears from the other direction. Taking in the mess and always appreciative of some bit of chaos to upset his master and brighten his own day, Launcelet can barely stifle his amusement at the disarray up and down the street. Shylock, with growing rage, snatches him by the ear and sends him with rebuke into the shop to fetch pail and brush to clean up the mess.

Launcelet re-emerges with utensils in hand and glumly sets about his task, while the neighbour invites Shylock to sit in the adjacent premises for a morning coffee. Almost as abruptly as his temper flared, Shylock returns to cordial conversation and a contemplative consideration with his chum of the state of business. Launcelet struggles with the remains of the Irgun poster, directing furtive glances towards his boss and muttering expletives under his breath.

Their coffee complete and his mood more tranquil, Shylock rises to return to his shop just as a contingent of Labour youth with their distinctive blue peasant shirts – red laced ties at the neck – work shorts and sandals energetically march through the square on a tour singing songs of the "the conquest of labour" (Kibbush Ha'avodah) and defiance of the British blockade. Shylock, whose world is business, not politics or pioneering, takes note of them without enthusiasm and returns to his shop barking new orders to Launcelet – his first mission of the day now complete.

As the lights slowly fade, we are suddenly aware of the presence of our three friends of the night before positioned in civilian garb in various guises around the square, observing we know not what ...

(Fade to black.)

1.2

Belmont House, Jerusalem.

Enter PORTIA with waiting-woman, NERISSA.

Portia's opening lines regarding her weary tiny physique are said with a certain irony since for our purposes she is anything but a "tiny body". She is a tall, lithesome, and attractive horsewoman (à la young Maggie Smith or Vanessa Redgrave) with an imposing air of intellectuality about her in the Bloomsbury mode. Her late father was a high-ranking military man and friend of General Allenby, and his military bearing has bequeathed her a certain "spine", despite lifestyle choices that run to the Bohemian. This physical and emotional bearing will aid Portia's masquerade later on as the judge, Balthasar, in the trial scene. She is very much a modern woman and feminist who feels with intensity the injustice of the constraints placed upon her by family obligation and position – a political disposition which ultimately makes her "fall" for Bassanio the more dramatic and amusing. Nerissa is her working-class lady-in-waiting and confidante, with whom she has become close and freely shares her inner-most feelings, especially about the follies of men. A perceptive woman of active intelligence (à la young Judi Dench or Joan Plowright), Nerissa aspires to the modern fashions of her mistress, but remains the more grounded of the two due to her working-class origins.

The scene opens with Portia partially wrapped (or unwrapped as the case may be) in a Turkish towel sprawled on an ornate oriental divan. She is receiving a deep and friendly massage from Nerissa who takes an obvious interest in her lithesome body and the effects of her techniques upon it. A half-read copy of Lawrence's *Women in Love*, dangles from Portia's limp, outstretched arm and falls to the floor.

Portia, sinking into her massage, indulges her feelings of weariness with the world, physically and emotionally.

Nerissa cautions her against self-pity, observing that she would be justified in such feelings if her misfortunes were as great as her advantages. But on the other hand, she observes, well-off people seem to suffer as much as the deprived, so it's best to be in between. Great wealth ages you faster, moderation helps you live longer. Portia commends her argument: good point, well made.

Nerissa presses her point further by asserting that her advice to Portia would be even better if applied to her life!

Portia responds, in effect, "easier said than done, my dear," and discourses philosophically on the problem of "practicing what one preaches". She notes that the brain can rationally tell the blood (and heart) what to do but hot emotions can overpower cold rationality, and the madness of youth is as agile as a hare leaping over the cripple, good advice. But she observes, this line of thinking is not going to help her "choose" a husband. And isn't the word "choosing", ironic, since she is not at liberty to either choose who she wants or reject who she doesn't want but must conform to the dictates of her late father? Isn't it oppressive, she laments, that she can neither choose nor refuse?

Nerissa tries to soothe her by recounting the virtues of Portia's father, who has imposed these strictures upon her, and invests his deathbed "inspirations" with mystical force. The candidate who wins the lottery for her hand by correctly choosing the meaning attached to the chests of gold, silver, and lead, must be her intended. No one will choose successfully, she believes, who won't love her truly. She then enquires how Portia feels about the suitors she's already seen.

Portia, already less than impressed by the hopefuls she's encountered, impishly invites Nerissa to play a little game: as Nerissa runs down the list, Portia will describe the suitor in personal detail and based upon her description Nerissa can guess what she thinks of them.

And so, they cattily begin cataloguing the "virtues" of the men come a-courtin':

The Neapolitan prince?
  Horse obsessed; his mother must have screwed a blacksmith!

The Count Pallatine?
  Obsessively morose! If he's this humourless now, what will he become when he gets older? Both are losers.

The French lord, M. le Bon?
  He's a man of sorts, but of indeterminate character. He's all things to all people and unpredictable. He tries to outdo everyone. It would be like marrying 20 men. She'd forgive him if he hated her, since she could never love him no matter how madly he loved her.

What about Falconbridge, the young English baron?
 No opinion, we can't communicate, we speak no common language. He's fine to look at, but how do you talk to a mime?! And his garments are bizarre, a motley of raiment from many lands, and his behaviour is even worse.

How about his neighbour, the Scottish lord?
 Rather forgiving since he suffered abuse at the hands of the Englishman and only threatened to strike back later. The Frenchman then offered to help him out against the English but abused him as well! (What a wimp!).

How do you like the Duke of Saxony's nephew?
 He's vile in the morning when he's sober, and vilest in the afternoon when he's drunk! At his best he's a little less than a man and at his worst he's little better than a beast. And if she became his widow, Nerissa adds provocatively, *she could surely get along without him! But if he were to choose the right casket and you still refuse him, you'd be violating your father's dying wish.*

Therefore, to avoid the worst, Portia instructs Nerissa to place a cup of white wine on the wrong casket. His addiction will rule his choice. She'll do anything rather than marry a drunk!

Coming back to reality, Nerissa reassures her that she needn't worry, she's spoken to all the prospects, and they're tired of the "choose-the-casket" game and want to return home, unless there's some other way to win her hand.

Portia proclaims her intention to remain a virgin into extreme old age unless she is wed according to her father's will. She is glad her wooers are reasonable enough to lose interest for there's not one of them she would waste time thinking about in their absence and wishes them bon voyage!

Nerissa now takes another tack, asking Portia if she remembers a young Venetian scholar and soldier in the entourage of the Marquess of Montferrat that she met when her father was alive?

Portia thinks she still remembers him by name, Bassanio.

Nerissa confirms that's the man and that he's the best "catch" she's ever seen.

The idea starts to dawn on Portia. She remembers him well and agrees with Nerissa's opinion of him.

But before the thought can develop further, the two are interrupted by the arrival of a servant who brings news that the four suitors are looking for her to say goodbye, and that a messenger from a new suitor, the Prince of Morocco, has arrived with word that the Prince will be arriving that night.

Portia declares that if she could be as happy about his approach as she is about the departure of the other four, she'd be delighted to receive him. But anticipating his race (which she apparently doesn't care for) Portia intimates that if he's as virtuous as a saint, but black like the devil, she'd rather confess to him than marry him. She bids Nerissa go with her, ordering the servant to go on ahead of them. As they exit, she remarks, facetiously, that as soon as one wooer departs another knocks on the door!

Exeunt.

1.3

Old City of Jerusalem, Shylock's office.

The audience sits for a beat in silence and darkness, which is suddenly broken by the beeping signal of Greenwich Mean Time (GMT), prelude to a BBC broadcast. Lights come up revealing the interior of Shylock's office near the Jaffa Gate in the Old City of Jerusalem. He is seated at his desk fiddling with his radio as Bassanio stands opposite him expectantly. He mutters, "Three thousand ducats, well" ... as he struggles to get clear reception. Bassanio is about to speak but is cut-off by a flicker of Shylock's finger as the news headlines suddenly trumpet the latest confrontations in Palestine between British Mandatory authorities and the growing resistance to the British blockade of refugees trying to reach safe haven there, followed by the immediately recognisable voice of Golda Meir addressing the 22nd Zionist Congress in Basle Switzerland. Her address, interrupted intermittently by poor reception brings their negotiations to a halt, much to Bassanio's frustration:

Voice of Golda Meir: ...Why are we now pressing our demand for a Jewish state ... as a desperate, immediate need? We understood this necessity the moment that we 600,000 Jews in Palestine ... stood powerless to rescue hundreds and thousands of Jews, perhaps millions, from certain death. The only obstacle between our readiness to rescue the Jews of Europe and the terrible certainty that death awaited them at Hitler's hands ... was a political regulation laid down by strangers - the White Paper! The

British government stood between us and millions of Jews lost in Europe...

Shylock's ruminations and Bassanio's pleadings resume haltingly, around continued attempts to get the latest news. The two carry on their haphazard and non-committal negotiations until Bassanio presses for his "answer", at which point Shylock starts to address him with greater focus, asserting that "Antonio is a good man". When Bassanio asks if he's heard anything to the contrary, Shylock flippantly dismisses such a thought. Rising from his chair he slowly ambles out the door of his office onto the square as he ruminates further on the state of Antonio's affairs. Bassanio follows impatiently in tow.

Emerging onto a small patio with tables and chairs, Shylock motions to Bassanio to sit and snaps for his assistant Launcelet to bring coffee for him and his guest. His manner is deliberate and studied. He reflects aloud on the intelligence he has of Antonio's ventures and the state of his finances. He speculates colourfully on where his argosies are headed and the myriad threats on land and sea that may await them. He manipulatively plays his cards close to the vest asserting his position as "top dog" in the negotiations by means of his reticence, all the while watching Bassanio squirm. After a thorough consideration of the perils of ships and sailors, rats and thieves, waters, winds and rocks, Shylock leads Bassanio further on by affirming that, all things considered, Antonio still looks like a good bet financially – good for the 3,000 ducats – and he just may take his bond for the loan.

Bassanio, eagerly assures him that Antonio is good for the money. To which Shylock retorts, with sudden vehemence, that he, indeed, will be assured before he makes any loan. And how he will be assured he must consider (i.e., deal not closed). He further pushes his advantage by requesting a face-to-face meeting with Antonio.

Bassanio, in a magnanimous faux pas (oblivious to Shylock's dietary restrictions) invites Shylock to dine with him and Antonio.

Incensed at what he assumes to be a "gracious" invitation to eat pork, Shylock dismisses the gesture with caustic allusion to the tale of Jesus casting-out demons into the bodies of swine, emphasising through Christian imagery his revulsion at the popular Christian fare. He makes it clear to Bassanio that he'll buy and sell, talk and walk with him, among other things, but he absolutely will not eat, drink, or pray with him. While amid this remonstrance, Shylock catches movement of an approaching figure whom he takes to be another merchant, and quickly enquires of him the news of the Rialto.

The figure is quickly introduced by Bassanio as none other than Antonio himself.

Shylock (to himself) reveals his pent-up animosity towards Antonio, "How like a fawning publican he looks" (What a snake in the grass he looks like). Shylock hates him because he's a "Goy" (with all that implies in Shylock's mind regarding the Christian antisemitism of the period from which he has amply suffered) and even more so because he maliciously undercuts interest rates in

Palestine by lending "gratis" which threatens Shylock's livelihood. Shylock vows that if he gets the chance, he'll make him pay for it. He views Antonio as a bigot of the first chop, who constantly humiliates him publicly in the Rialto, his place of business, in front of his colleagues – ranting against him, his bargains and his well-earned profits, which Antonio disparages as "interest". It would be a curse upon the Hebrew nation if he were to forgive the man.

Bassanio interrupts his vengeful fantasies, asking if he's listening.

Shylock, without missing a beat and ignoring Antonio as if he were not present, snaps back to his prior negotiating tactics claiming that his thoughts were preoccupied with an assessment of his present finances. And, to tell the truth, as best he can recall, he doesn't have the full 3,000 ducats at hand at the moment. But... "What does it matter?" Shylock declares ingratiatingly, Tubal, a wealthy Jewish friend will back him (no problem!). But hold on, he manipulatively queries of Bassanio (as if he hadn't heard before), how many months do you want the loan for?

Suddenly, as if for the first time, Shylock acknowledges the presence of Antonio, who has been observing the discussion. He greets him unctuously as if his sudden presence is a great surprise and what a coincidence since they were just speaking about him!

Antonio declares defensively, with misgivings, that although he never lends or borrows with interest, as a rule, he's willing to make an exception in this case to serve the needs of his friend (which is the only reason he's there). Bypassing Shylock, he enquires of Bassanio if Shylock knows how much he needs?

Shylock interjects, "yes, yes, 3,000 ducats".

Antonio makes clear, "for three months".

Shylock, feigning apology, responds that he had forgotten, and switching focus to Bassanio (thereby dividing the two negotiators) affirms, ingratiatingly, that he did tell him that.

Back to Antonio, Shylock takes up the matter of the guarantee… but catches himself up short recalling Antonio's claim that he never lends nor borrows with interest.

Antonio confirms that he's right, he never uses it.

To overcome this "objection", Shylock digresses from the negotiations with a roundabout defence of his lending practices by way of a Biblical allegory about Jacob and his uncle Laban's sheep, which he renders in convoluted and seemingly irrelevant detail confusing the discussion and Antonio.

Shylock relates how Jacob devised a tactic of inducing the birth of spotted lambs in the ewes under his charge (which he was promised by Laban would be his) thereby legitimately expanding his business. It was a way to thrive and was a blessing, and there's nothing wrong with such devices and profits if the proceeds are not stolen.

Antonio, irritably rebuts Shylock's argument, asserting that the success of Jacob's business venture was God's will not his doing since Jacob had no control over the outcome. Is Shylock trying to say by this analogy that charging interest is a good thing? Does he think his gold and silver are ewes and rams?

Shylock parries by responding with a bad joke: he cannot tell (if his gold and silver are ewes and rams) – (but) he makes his profits breed as fast! Changing the subject, "But note me, signor…"

Antonio having none of Shylock's shenanigans, remarks to Bassanio to observe how the devil can manipulate holy writ to serve his purposes, comparing such an evil soul quoting holy scripture to a smiling villain - good looking on the outside but like a bad apple rotten to the core. Derisively asserting, what an attractive veneer dishonesty can have!

Shylock ignores his slights and returns to his studied calculations, stating once again that 3,000 ducats is a nice round sum and starts to calculate the interest for three months out of twelve.

Impatiently, Antonio demands to know if he's finally decided.

Shylock, who all this while has tried to adhere to a strategy of calculation and restraint, can do so no more. His true feelings and underlying resentments suddenly surge to the surface. He reminds Antonio of the many times he has humiliated and abused him in the Rialto, his place of business – insulting his money and business practices. Up 'til now he declares, he has borne these insults with forbearance because that is the lot of Jews in the Christian world!

He confronts Antonio with the vile insults he has subjected him to, reviling his faith, calling him a vicious dog, and spitting upon his

Jewish attire – and all because he lends his own money for profit. He further confronts Antonio with the supreme irony that now he needs his help and comes to him demanding money!

Shylock makes clear to Antonio the gall of his position – look who's now demanding money: the man who spit upon his beard (his very person and another symbol of his Jewishness) and kicked him like he would a stray dog out his door. Money is what he wants? (What nerve!)

Shylock derisively confronts Antonio with the perversity of his position: what can be said to him? Do dogs have money? Is it possible for "a cur" to lend 3000 ducats?!! Or should he bow low and in a servile mien recount the many times he's been insulted and conclude that for these acts of "kindness" he'll give him the money he desires?

Antonio, unrepentant and fully confirmed in his bigotry, tells Shylock to his face that as far as he's concerned, he'd do it all again, and not to do him any favours. Don't lend money to him as if he were his friend – since when do friends charge each other interest, anyway? But lend him the money as an enemy to make it easier to impose the penalty if he should forfeit the loan.

Shylock abruptly changes tack, trying to outwit Antonio's bile. Why is he getting so riled up about things, he reproaches him? He just wants to be friends with Antonio, put all the hard feelings behind them and provide him with the resources he needs without a penny of interest – but he laments, Antonio just won't listen. This is an act of kindness he's offering!

Bassanio is momentarily convinced and concurs that Shylock's offer seems genuine.

Shylock now displays a contradictory tendency often seen in victims of oppression. Despite his deep-seated resentment of Antonio and his abuse, he has a perverse desire to ingratiate himself, to be accepted by him, even to be liked by his abuser, if it's possible. He then proceeds with his show of magnanimity, further embellishing his offer in a manner bordering on the ridiculous.

He proposes that they go straightway to a notary and seal Antonio's bond, and if against all odds he can't pay back the loan according to the specifications of the contract, then he'll have to forfeit (let's think of something ridiculous)... Okay, a pound of his flesh cut from anywhere that Shylock desires (what could be more implausible, if not idiotic, than that, eh?).

Antonio is suddenly amused and convinced of Shylock's sincerity by this extravagant appeal. (Who, after all, would propose a bond as improbable of collection as to amount to no bond at all, if he wasn't truly generous? It's virtually free money!) He suddenly changes heart, accepts the deal and even proclaims that "the Jew" isn't so bad after all!

But Bassanio suddenly gets "cold feet" dissuading Antonio from such a bargain and declaring he'd rather go without the money than see him placed in such jeopardy, no matter how improbable. But Antonio, now enthralled with a sense of irrational optimism at the prospect of such a bargain, tells Bassanio not to worry, that within two months – and a month before the deadline – he'll have cargoes returned worth three times the price of the bond.

Shylock, observing the wrangling between these two "friends", and yet still desirous of a minor victory in the form of a cordial pact with his oppressors, shakes his head in dismay at these "Goyim", who project their own suspicions onto the motives of others. He impresses upon the squabbling pair that the proposed bond of a pound of human flesh is absurd and worthless to him. What could he possibly gain by collecting it? It's not worth the meat of sheep, beef, or goats!

In a final move to close the deal, Shylock, professes to lose patience with further indecision. He asserts with recrimination that he's making this ludicrous offer, that gains him nothing financially, in the hope that it might buy the good favour of Antonio. If he takes it, fine. If not, adieu! And hopefully there'll be no hard feelings.

Antonio is sold, he'll take the deal and agree to its terms.

Clearly pleased, Shylock quickly instructs them to go directly to the notary and inform him of their "silly" bargain while he goes to collect the money and check on the condition of his house which he left in charge of his unreliable shop assistant Launcelet, after which he'll be with them straight away.

Antonio encourages his new "Jewish friend" to make haste.

Exit SHYLOCK.

He then jests condescendingly to Bassanio that Shylock has become so kind that he's now almost a Christian!

Bassanio, with lingering foreboding, declares that he doesn't like the combination of good intentions and a villain's mind.

Antonio brushes aside his misgivings, insisting that there's nothing to worry about, his ships will arrive a month before the deadline.

Exeunt.

[1.3a – insert]

Shylock's Office – Interior – Shylock's Dream Sequence

With resignation and disdain, Shylock retreats from his encounter with Antonio to his lair, his private office where his most serious work is done.

In effort to relieve his agitation and resentment, Shylock throws himself into inspection of his ledgers. The work grows increasingly tedious. Bored by his endless lists, he shunts aside the books with a hint of distaste and reaches into his desk to retrieve an aged and ornately-bound copy of the Tanakh (Bible). His countenance softens as he delicately holds the holy book before his face perusing it as if lovingly examining the face of a woman. He kisses the text and gently places it before him on the desk opening it to his current portion, Ketuvim (Writings) and the "Song of Songs", which he has bookmarked. He begins to recite, "Hinach yaffa raiyati, hinach yaffa. Hinach yaffa, eynaich yonim…" ("Behold, how beautiful you are, my love. Behold, how beautiful! Your eyes are doves" …). His face grows soft with a compassion and love long suppressed, his eyes well with tears, as his heart fills haltingly with a passion long dormant but not forgotten. It is longing for Leah, his beloved, whose eyes, like doves, beckon him from his worldly purgatory. He begins to dream, he swoons, his head slowly falling to the desk, lights dimming.

As the lights around Shylock dim, the sound of a beautiful Greek/Ladino lullaby is heard and a spot slowly comes up on a *beautiful, dark-haired Leah, singing to her young daughter Jessica, who is in a cradle. Suddenly, Shylock is young again and sweeps Leah to him in a beautifully-choreographed Greek couple dance in which the two, locked in shared passion, reflect the glory of his youth. But suddenly the music turns, as balletically the story tells poignantly of Leah's affliction and ultimate death from breast cancer (à la ballet,* La Dame aux Camélias, *by John Neumeier with music by Frédéric Chopin, created for Marcia Haydée).*

The couple is devastatingly parted by the figure of death and the scene transformed to her graveside where Shylock stands holding Jessica tightly in unrelieved grief. Suddenly, partisans arrive with frantic warning that the Nazi invasion of Salonika has begun, and they must flee immediately. Shylock, paralysed with longing for Leah, still warm in her grave, is removed bodily by his compatriots as he reaches for her, his final farewell untimely ended.

As in the logic of a dream the image of Leah and the young Jessica re-emerges. The distant melody is heard again – the lovely voice of Leah, cradling their daughter, Jessica, at bedtime. Shylock, seen in silhouette at the table, lifts his head in longing struggling to raise his body from the desk and reach out to the pair. The mother and child take note of him across a divide that can never be breached. They smile lovingly, the little girl outstretching her arms towards her father. Shylock struggles, arms like lead, to reach out to them and join their loving song. The tableau is held with agonising intensity for several beats. Then the singing of mother and child dies away, the two slowly vanishing like the ghost of Hamlet's father at the approaching dawn.

Shylock collapses on the desk sobbing in his sleep. Slowly, painfully he awakens, rises, and staggers towards the door in a state of utter desolation.

Exit SHYLOCK.

ACT TWO

2.1

Belmont House Banqueting Hall, a raucous costume party in progress.

Portia, caught between her family obligations and her rebellious nature, and mindful of her status and gossip value among the "smart-set", has decided to "send-up" the husband-finding ritual for public consumption. She has organised a soirée at Belmont House attended by a pot-pourri of high society entertained by a small jazz orchestra, the scene rife with sexual intrigue and gossip.

The room is filled with those of her inner circle: a Bloomsbury-type crowd of dissolute poets, socially awkward philosophers and social critics making inept and self-conscious effort to play the role of fun-seeking party-goers, among a more uninhibited and lively contingent of assorted upper-crust exotics in costumes and masks, ranging from the humorous to the provocative – women in tuxedos, men in togas, a beefy, square-jawed police commander decked-out in a long gown and jewels like a monstrous Margaret Dumont (of Marx Brothers' fame) ostentatiously wielding a cigarette holder of prodigious length and grinning with self-satisfaction, etc.

In addition, Mandatory military and diplomatic officials, Arab dignitaries, and certain identifiably foreign figures of mystery (most likely the remains of wartime Nazi agents still working on behalf of the Palestinians, Syrians, and Iraqis) round-out the gathering.

Gratiano enters upstage, in animated and ingratiating conversation with an Arab notable. Observing two German guests engaged in muted conversation taking in the scene, he immediately recognises the taller of the two: a gaunt, austere Prussian of military bearing. He signals to him and rushes to introduce his Arab companion. He looks on congenially as they exchange introductions, punctuated by reflexive heel clicks from the German. The two quickly engage in friendly conversation and move to less public quarters off-stage for further talks.

Nerissa, in blue-green grease paint, sparkles, and tights, flits about the room like a demonic Puck, dashes to a door, *UC*, pokes her head out and confers with someone on the other side. She then swiftly re-enters and dashes across the room to the bandleader and whispers in his ear, who abruptly breaks off the music leaving the dance floor in a state of momentary confusion.

Suddenly, the crowd's attention is caught by a loud drum-roll as the brass of the ensemble launches into the overture to Handel's, *Royal Fireworks Suite*. The crowd is perplexed and electrified by the sudden change in repertoire and its rising anticipation is met with the sudden flinging open of the doors revealing Portia dressed in a long trench-coat with large sunglasses posing, Garbo-like, in the doorway.

She enters dramatically and sashays through the adoring crowd in time to the fanfare that, applauding, makes way for her. Portia arrives at an elevated platform with a large piece of furniture covered by a batik of Turkish design. She poses for a beat dramatically before flinging off her trench-coat and glasses revealing a stunning diaphanous gown which renders her, Titania-like, the perfect complement to Nerissa's Puck. The audience roars approvingly. Nerissa, true to her character, flies up to the platform behind her and with exaggerated ceremony, like a magician's assistant, swiftly removes the batik cover revealing a throne-like chair of Eastern design with a plush pillow. Portia regally takes her seat to the delight of her guests.

Flourish of cornets. Nerissa flies off the platform and commands centre stage. Turning towards the doors upstage she grandly gestures and announces: "His Majesty, the Prince of Morocco!"

("Enter the Prince of Morocco, a tawny Moor all in white and three or four followers accordingly...")

Morocco, a dark and exotic man senses he is out of place here, but confident of his worth, and humorously over-confident of his virility, he proceeds optimistically towards his expected conquest.

Nerissa has quickly returned to Portia's side by her throne. The two of them, suddenly intrigued by the sight of Morocco, despite initial misgivings, subtly exchange glances while the assembled guests are abuzz with a variety of reactions and comments.

Morocco picks up on their reactions and interprets them to imply objection to his race. In effort to overcome this obstacle to his candidacy, Morocco takes the initiative to boastfully explain that his outward colour is simply the product of living in the sun, but that his blood flows red as any man's. Bring him the handsomest Northerner and he'll cut himself to prove his blood is redder, if that will win her. What is more, his colour makes the valiant fear him and the girls back home love him. He wouldn't change it except to steal her thoughts.

Portia, diplomatically, and somewhat disingenuously, explains to him (and her audience) that looks aren't everything, that there are other considerations that may win a maid's heart. In any event, it doesn't matter here for she is obliged to follow the dictates of the lottery imposed upon her by the wishes of her late father, so she isn't free to choose. But she graciously reassures him, if not for that restriction, his personal attributes would stand him in as good stead to win her affection as any she has yet seen.

Morocco thanks her, profusely, for even her modest attention, and runs down a list of heroic and dangerous deeds of Herculean dimensions he would perform if he might win her. But is then brought up short by the prospect that mere chance ("blind fortune") – a force beyond his control and insensitive to his many virtues – might ultimately deny him in favour of an "unworthier man", to let him die in grief.

Portia seizes her out and lays down the rules to her "tawny" suitor: he's got to take his chances; either don't choose at all or swear that if he chooses wrongly, he'll never speak of marriage again with any woman – so he had best think carefully.

Morocco takes up the dare and requests that he take his chance.

Portia prolongs the drama by suggesting dinner first, and then on to his game of chance.

Morocco optimistically embraces his fate which will make him either the most blessed or cursed among men!

The band strikes up the Handel *Finale* and the two exit with the titillated crowd all abuzz in tow.

Exeunt.

2.2

An Arab café, Old City of Jerusalem.

We find Launcelet Gobbo in animated conversation with a group of friends in a café in the Old City of Jerusalem sitting at austere tables smoking and drinking Turkish coffee. A larger contingent of habitués playing "shesh besh" periodically look on. Launcelet is unusually animated amidst the largely sullen crowd and commands centre stage as he satirically relates the latest gossip about the Jews, in particular relating to his master, Shylock. His style as raconteur is that of a stand-up comedian as he improvises with growing hilarity a see-saw debate between himself and the devil urging him, against his conscience, to flee his master Shylock, whom he describes, much to the pleasure and prejudices of his audience, as "the very devil incarnation". As his debate shifts back and forth, Launcelet peppers his narrative with off-colour remarks about his own father's infidelities and finally builds his routine to the climax that he's at the devil's disposal and will flee Shylock's service if he gives his command.

The previously subdued gathering is now in a state of raucous revelry when there suddenly enters, much to Launcelet's surprise, the elder Gobbo, his father, the very man whose honour he has just besmirched. Launcelet, still high on performance adrenaline and eager to cover his faux pas (and not knowing how much of It he's heard) continues incorporating his father's entrance into his routine.

As luck would have it, Old Gobbo is largely blind but has been attracted to the establishment by the sound of the gathering. He seeks directions to Shylock's house where he expects to find his son, unaware that Launcelet is the person he is addressing. In keeping with his irreverent attitude towards his father, Launcelet decides to have a little fun with the "old man" and gives him a convoluted set of directions to Shylock's house which he can't possibly follow. He perversely engages Old Gobbo in an animated discussion about himself which confirms him in the belief that he is not talking to his son, and then reverses field to convince him that he is.

Once his identity is declared, Launcelet abandons his routine and moves off centre stage with his father towards the door as the conversation becomes more serious. Finally, the old man is convinced that he is, indeed, talking with his son and remarks upon how much he's changed. Launcelet bemoans his state and avers he is being starved in his service to Shylock and is about to run away. When his father mentions that he came bearing a gift for Shylock, the son declares resentfully that if he wants to give Shylock a gift, he should give him a noose with which to hang himself! Better he should give Launcelet the gift for use as an inducement to Bassanio to take him into his service, since he treats his servants well and dresses them handsomely. Failing that, he'll run to the ends of the earth.

As the two exit to the street, they encounter the very Bassanio who is the object of Launcelet's designs giving instructions to an attendant regarding the delivery of certain letters, the making of uniforms, and an invitation to meet soon with Gratiano.

Launcelet pushes his father to approach Bassanio in hopes of enticing him to take him into his service. There then ensues a garbled "two-handed" interchange, as humorous in its ineptitude as the previous stand-up routine, in effort to alternatively explain Launcelet's estrangement from Shylock and to grease Bassanio's palm, as it were, and interest him in Launcelet as an assistant.

Losing patience with their ham-handed efforts at ingratiation, Bassanio demands they "cut to the chase", speak one at a time, and demands to know what they want.

Forced by the necessity to be concise, Launcelet declares his desire to serve Bassanio. Much to his amazement he is greeted with an immediate offer of employment. Bassanio indicates that he knows all about him and was, in fact, approached by Shylock that very day who recommended Launcelet to his service (apparently to get him off his hands). But it's all up to Launcelet who is more than willing. Bassanio instructs him and his father to formally take leave of Shylock and to find his lodgings, ordering his attendants to give his new recruit an especially nice uniform, and to be sure it is done.

Launcelet Gobbo, now beside himself with glee and self-congratulations, rhetorically repudiates the negative assessments of his employability and articulateness, proclaiming his luck, and a triumphant future written in his palm; a life-line boasting of sexual triumphs ranging from at least 15 wives, eleven widows, and nine maids (for starters!); escape from catastrophes involving three near-drownings and being caught in flagrante delicto with another man's wife (he points to smaller hand lines ensuring that escape), and declares that "if Fortune be a woman", she's good at this line of work! He calls his father to come along, and declares he'll now leave "the Jew" in the "twinkling" of an eye!

Launcelet and Old Gobbo exit, leaving Bassanio to attend uninterrupted to the evening's preparations with his servant Leonardo.

Bassanio engages Leonardo to rapidly purchase certain items he's listed in anticipation of his meeting with a person of importance that evening and to hurry back. Leonardo hastily sets off to do his bidding, almost colliding with the entrance of Gratiano who is clearly eager to engage Bassanio for reasons of his own. Gratiano, eager to find Bassanio, brushes off Leonardo's fumbling and demands of him where he can be found. Leonardo indicates Bassanio standing some distance away obscured by a pillar and exits as Gratiano loudly calls out to him.

Gratiano, summoning up as much sleazy charm as he can muster, energetically descends on Bassanio with the intention of soliciting a "favour" from him. Bassanio, buoyant with excitement and anticipation of the good fortune he is sure will await his pursuit of Portia, responds reflexively and magnanimously, "You have obtained it!"

Gratiano, aware he is treading on thin ice, puckishly demands, "You must not deny me, I must go with you to Belmont!"

Bassanio, still flush with optimism, is suddenly aware of the possible difficulties his downscale "friend's" presence may present in the elite environment of Belmont. He admonishes him, diplomatically, that sometimes his behaviour is on the crude side, and while this may be perfectly acceptable among "the boys" back home, it could prove disastrous to his chances in the environs of Belmont. Bassanio, however, agrees to take Gratiano with him on the condition that he applies "some cold drops of modesty" on his "skipping spirit" and "wild behaviour".

Gratiano swears an elaborate oath that he will behave soberly and with all civility, observing every manner of respectful discourse (and only swearing "but now and then"), and if he doesn't, "never trust (him) more"! To which Bassanio conditionally assents, declaring, "Well, we will see your bearing".

But Gratiano, in anticipation of the night's planned revelries, declares a last-minute caveat, "Nay, but I bar tonight. You shall not gauge me by what we do tonight." To which Bassanio readily agrees that it would be a pity for Gratiano to deny himself the pleasure of carousing in the company of friends assembled for that purpose – indeed, he should make every effort to enjoy himself.

Their "negotiations" complete, Bassanio declares his need to attend to other business and exits, while Gratiano declares his intention "to go to Lorenzo and the rest", and exits, as well.

2.3

Shylock's House.

Enter JESSICA and LAUNCELET.

Launcelet enters eagerly assembling his personal belongings for departure to his new master, Bassanio, with Jessica in tow. She is clearly agitated, both in response to Launcelet's departure as well as her own imminent escape from a house she describes as "hell". In a moment of compassion, she thanks Launcelet for his merry pranks which have provided some relief from her tedious existence there. She gifts him a ducat and requests that he secretly deliver a letter to Lorenzo, guest of his new master Bassanio, whom he will soon see at dinner. She then hurriedly bids him farewell for fear of being seen by Shylock.

Overcome by a rare moment of true affection penetrating his mask of cynicism and jocularity, Launcelet declares that his tears demonstrate his feelings. He tearfully bids Jessica farewell, pronouncing her his "most beautiful pagan" and "sweet Jew", who, if she'll not be the prize of some Christian knave, he'll be "much deceived". But getting a grip on himself and needing to flee the house, Launcelet thinks better of his unmanly display of emotion and bids her a final adieu. And Jessica, full of emotion, sees him off.

Exit LAUNCELET.

Alone and suddenly facing the implications of her rage towards her father, Jessica is overcome by self-recrimination and shame that she is guilty of the "sin" of being "ashamed to be (her) father's child". But she emphatically justifies her intended betrayal of Shylock declaring herself "daughter to his blood … not to his manners" and avowing that if "Lorenzo will keep (his) promise, (she) will end this strife, become a Christian and (his) loving wife".

Exit JESSICA.

2.4

An army barracks

Enter GRATIANO, LORENZO, SALARIO and SOLANIO.

The comrades enter in animated discussion of preparation for the night's revelries while taking up chores around the barracks.

Lorenzo animatedly lays out a plan to "slink away" at suppertime, change into costumes at his lodgings and return within an hour. Gratiano, however, is sceptical, objecting that they haven't yet made adequate preparations for their clandestine exploits.

Salario adds further objection that they haven't arranged yet for the indispensable torchbearers, and his sidekick, Solanio, pours further cold water on the proceedings by pessimistically declaring that unless deftly organised the masquerade could prove a disaster – in which case, better "not undertook".

Lorenzo, intent on his mission, dismisses their misgivings, insisting that they have two hours – more than ample time to prepare. Amid his brief, Lorenzo is interrupted by the sudden appearance of Launcelet who has tracked him down in earnest effort to deliver the secret letter from Jessica. He greets him, enquiring, "what's the news?"

Launcelet, ever the clown, jocularly quips that if he doesn't mind opening the letter, which he ceremoniously hands him, he'll find out soon enough! Lorenzo is immediately overcome by the sight of Jessica's handwriting, whose hand, he muses, is a beautiful hand, whiter than the paper she has written on.

Gratiano crudely breaks his reverie, licentiously enquiring if he's got a love letter. At which point, Launcelet tries, diplomatically, to exit the scene. Lorenzo enquires of him where he is headed, to which Launcelet replies he is going to Shylock's house to extend an invitation to dinner from his new master, Bassanio.

Lorenzo bids Launcelet wait. Pressing money in his palm, he enlists him in an additional service; to convey a message privately to Jessica in answer to her letter, that "(he) won't fail her". He then bids his comrades go and prepare for the evening's festivities, declaring suggestively, he has his torchbearer!

Exit LAUNCELET.

Solanio and Salario are now one with the plan. Lorenzo bids them meet at Gratiano's house in an hour's time, which they agree to do, Salario declaring "tis good we do so".

Exit SALARIO and SOLANIO.

Gratiano, probingly enquires if the letter Lorenzo has just received is from Jessica?

Lorenzo, with growing intensity, declares to Gratiano that he must tell him "all". Jessica, in her letter, has revealed to him how to liberate her from her father's house, what gold and silver she possesses, and detailed the page's suit she will wear as a disguise to make their getaway.

Overcome with anticipation of his hoped-for romantic triumph, Lorenzo, nonetheless, reveals his ingrained bigotry towards the very people from which his love-interest derives, declaring derisively that if "the Jew", her father, ever gets to heaven, it will be because of her virtues, and, conversely, if any bad luck befalls her, it will be because "... she is issue to a faithless Jew".

In haste, Lorenzo bids Gratiano accompany him and offers him the letter to read as they go, declaring triumphantly: "Fair Jessica shall be my torchbearer".

Exeunt.

2.5

Shylock's House

Enter SHYLOCK and LAUNCELET.

Shylock enters in the company of Launcelet, now his ex-employee, agitated and ambivalent about the dinner invitation he has brought. Still berating him as if he never left his employ, Shylock admonishes Launcelet that he will no longer be living the life of Riley as he has done under his roof, stuffing himself, sleeping and snoring, and wearing out his clothes. Amid his distracted scolding, Shylock repeatedly calls for Jessica, a call taken up mockingly by Launcelet as well, which succeeds admirably in getting Shylock's goat! Peeved by Launcelet's presumption, Shylock demands to know who asked him for his "services", to which Launcelet declares in triumph that Shylock always told him he couldn't do anything without being told, a condition now belied by his newly acquired independence. At which point Jessica enters, inquiring about the purpose of Shylock's call to her.

Shylock, now preoccupied on several fronts, begins to explain that he has been invited to supper and gives Jessica his keys for safe keeping. But no sooner does he do so, than he ambivalently questions his plan, declaring dismissively that he has not been invited to Bassanio's "for love", but rather for flattery. Yet, just as rapidly he resolves his internal debate, asserting that if he can't go for love, he can, at least, follow through for spite, and take advantage of "the prodigal Christian". He instructs Jessica with due gravity to watch and secure the house. Still wracked by uncertainty even as he methodically organises his departure, Shylock fleetingly interrupts his progress to express feelings of unease and lack of desire to set forth made the more pronounced by the ill-omen he has had in the form of a dream of "money bags" the night before.

Seeing his reluctance, and eager to move the elopement "conspiracy" along, Launcelet nervously encourages his departure, ineptly reminding him, by way of his penchant for malaprop, that Bassanio imminently expects his "reproach" (approach). Shylock pointedly picks up on the slip, retorting caustically, "so do I (expect) his (reproach)!", to which Launcelet, in a state of growing agitation at the passing time, inadvertently blurts out that "they have conspired together" – almost spilling the beans about the plans underway – before catching himself mid-sentence and covering his near faux pas with a stream of blather, parodying Shylock, about a premonition he had, with accompanying physical ailments, predicting a masquerade party – which might or might not happen – but if it does, "you heard it here first!"

Launcelet's line of rubbish nearly spills the beans a second time. But the mention of masques suddenly deflects Shylock's attention from the discussion at hand, piquing his ire and setting him off on a rant fired by repugnance at the "degenerate" Christian mores such ribald entertainments represent.

During his choler, Shylock's attention is suddenly turned to his daughter, Jessica, and the security of his home. In the sad but all too common way that authoritarian parents often displace their anxieties and fears onto the shoulders of the children they wish to protect, Shylock, with sudden hostility, admonishes Jessica – as if the impending threat were hers - not to look out the window at the "Christian fools with varnished faces" in the streets, and to stop-up the ears of his "sober house" lest it be defiled by "the sound of shallow foppery". Shylock's reprimand – which takes on growing and intimidating proportions fuelled by long-simmering resentments against the Christian world around him – is the irrational flip side of his deep love for his daughter, Jessica; a love he cannot properly express being distorted and inhibited by years of fearful obsessions and the unresolved loss of her mother, Leah.

Jessica's understandable resentment at this treatment is writ large emotionally, and perceived by Shylock as an act of defiance which further fuels his instability and growing rage. In a sudden fit of pique, his demons take control of him. He snaps and, acting out of all proportion, slaps Jessica for her perceived insolence. The shock of this moment suddenly halts Shylock's tirade. The two stand transfixed: joined and, at the same time, critically divided in pain and silence as Jessica weeps nursing the wound to her cheek. A deep but unarticulated remorse flashes across Shylock's face. Evading responsibility for his abuse and shame, he adopts an air of glib denial, abruptly returning to the question of his departure, as if nothing had happened. Threatening once again not to leave, he vacillates yet again, finally ordering Launcelet to go forth with the news that he will, indeed, come.

Launcelet declares to Shylock that he will go, and cryptically encourages Jessica to defy Shylock's orders and watch for a certain "Christian", who'll be by and "worth a Jewesses eye" – the saviour who may liberate her from her travails.

Shylock, still decompressing from his diatribe, doesn't catch Launcelet's comments to Jessica and enquires of her what he has just said. Jessica tells him that Launcelet simply said, "'Farewell, mistress', nothing else". Shylock, in ongoing denial of his abusive behaviour, evasively takes up an assessment of Launcelet's "virtues", declaring him to be a "nice enough" fool, slow as a snail in industry, sleeping by day like a wildcat, and unproductive as a drone in a beehive. Which is why he's more than happy to dispense with him so he can waste his new master's money; monies, which Shylock caustically notes with pleasure, that Bassanio has just borrowed from him.

With a hesitant display of affection, trying to paper-over the damage he's done, Shylock kisses Jessica on the cheek and gazes at her for a fleeting moment before instructing her to go into the interior of the house, reassuring her – much to her dismay – that he may, in any event, return shortly, and re-emphasising the need to secure the house and lock all the doors, crowning his directives with the inane maxim, "Fast bind, fast find. A proverb never stale in thrifty mind."

Exit SHYLOCK.

Watching him depart, Jessica – burning with resentment – declares goodbye, expressing the hope that if her luck proves true, she will soon lose a father and he a daughter, too.

Exit.

2.6

A street outside Shylock's house

Enter the masquers GRATIANO and SALARIO.

Gratiano enters provocatively decked out in a black military-style tunic of a Mosleyite fascist, accompanied by Salario sporting a large-nosed Pantalone mask and commedia costume, suggestive of Shylock himself.

Gratiano recognises Shylock's house where their meeting with Lorenzo is to take place. Salario remarks, worriedly, that he's late. Gratiano agrees that it's strange he hasn't made their rendezvous on time since lovers tend to be early rather than late, and Salario humorously notes that very time runs ten times faster for new lovers than for those long wed.

Not to be outdone, Gratiano bloviates on the natural order of things that makes young love the more intense; citing the all too obvious facts that an appetite sated at a meal is not as intense as it was before eating, a horse cannot retrace his trail with the same energy he had when starting out, all things in life are pursued with greater energy than they are enjoyed once acquired, and how majestically a ship sets sail buoyed gently by the winds only to return the weather-beaten and threadbare victim of those same winds at sea.

At which point Salario cuts short Gratiano's long-winded speech as the tardy Lorenzo appears.

Enter LORENZO.

Lorenzo, out of breath and flush with anticipation, apologises and thanks them for their patience, claiming that not he but "pressing affairs" caused his delay, quipping suggestively that when, in future, they too must steal their own wives, he'll wait just as long for them! He hurriedly motions them over beneath the nearby balcony which he identifies, somewhat ironically, as the home of "the Jew", his father-in-law to be. He calls out, "who's within"?

Enter JESSICA above, disguised as a boy.

Jessica emerges onto the balcony disguised as a boy. She calls out to Lorenzo, whose voice she recognises, to confirm his identity to be sure it is him. Lorenzo responds, he is her love, and she, caught up in the passion of her love requited and dream fulfilled, fervently acknowledges his identity, and affirms his vow "... For who love I so much?", as only he knows. Lorenzo returns her vows, declaring that heaven and her thoughts are witness to his love.

Jessica suddenly turns to the practical business at hand throwing down to him a casket which she suggestively proclaims will be "worth the pains". Suddenly, self-conscious, and ashamed of her disguise as a boy, Jessica declares it fortunate that it is night so no one can see the "pretty follies" committed in the name of love. But, she rationalises, "love is blind", and lovers cannot see the foolishness in which they indulge, for if they could, "Cupid himself would blush to see me thus transformèd to a boy."

Lorenzo calls for her to descend from the balcony to be his torchbearer, as per their planned escape. Jessica, with growing ambivalence about the tactics employed, demurs, objecting that her behaviour is already too flagrantly immodest and observable and shouldn't be further illuminated. While in the guise of a torchbearer, she should be concealed.

Lorenzo reassures her that she is concealed in the lovely disguise of a boy, but insists they must make haste, for time flies at night and they are late for Bassanio's feast.

Jessica, overcoming her inhibitions, tells Lorenzo she will join him straightaway after snatching some more ducats and locking-up the house.

Exit JESSICA above.

Gratiano, who has been taking in the scene all the while in his Oswald Mosley getup, cynically quips that Jessica exhibits all the qualities "of a gentle and no Jew!"

Lorenzo, thoroughly besotted, ignores his jibe and waxes poetic about her virtues, declaring her, in his judgment, to be wise, beautiful, and faithful. And if she remains so, she will always have a place in his soul.

Enter JESSICA.

Jessica suddenly rushes forth from the house. They confront each other with wild anticipation. The world stops. They passionately embrace. Lorenzo breaks away, commanding with authority his comrades onward to meet their "masquing mates" now awaiting them.

Exit LORENZO with JESSICA and SALARIO.

Enter ANTONIO.

Hard on the heels of their exit, Antonio hurriedly enters the street calling out to the figure of Gratiano, "who's there?" Gratiano responds uncertainly, recognising his voice from a distance. Antonio swiftly descends upon him demanding to know where everyone is, berating him that all their friends are waiting for them and informing him that the masque has been cancelled. The winds have suddenly changed, Bassanio will be setting sail forthwith, and he's sent twenty men out looking for him!

Gratiano, grown bored with the evening's foppery and eager for some manly action, expresses his pleasure at the prospect of being under sail and gone from the scene that night. They rapidly exit to their destinations.

Exeunt.

2.7

Belmont House Banqueting Hall

Flourish cornets. Enter PORTIA with the Prince of MOROCCO, and their trains.

Portia, Morocco, and their respective entourages return from dinner to the main hall with the crowd of guests excitedly surging in behind them, jockeying for position to see the "choose-the-casket" competition. Portia ceremoniously instructs her servant to draw a curtain revealing three caskets of gold, silver, and lead for the Prince's inspection.

She invites Morocco now to make his choice.

Morocco approaches the caskets accompanied by two ominous-looking slave bodyguards. Each has a cryptic inscription upon it which he reads and ponders: Gold: "Who chooseth me shall gain what many men desire." Silver: "Who chooseth me shall get as much as he deserves." Lead: "Who chooseth me must give and hazard all he hath."

Morocco, growing tense with anticipation asks how he will know if he chooses correctly, to which Portia replies that the right casket contains her picture, and if he chooses the right one both she and the picture are his.

Morocco implores the aid of Allah and contemplates the inscriptions yet again. He concludes, first off, that the lead casket offers no enticing prospect, suggesting, as it does, that he must risk all for lead – something which a man of his "golden mind" and standing would not do in hopes of receiving something worthless. He moves on to the silver casket whose motto initially attracts him, convinced as he is that a man of his lineage, wealth, graces, breeding, and especially love, indeed, "deserves" Portia. But he is suddenly given pause by doubt. What if his self-proclaimed virtues are not, in fact, sufficient to claim her – what then? Perhaps, he should consider the gold casket before making his decision.

The casket declares: "Who chooseth me shall gain what many men desire" – the perfect evocation of Portia. He waxes poetic about the vast expanses that men travel in pursuit of Portia – "to kiss this shrine, this mortal breathing saint" – from the deserts and "vasty wilds of wide Arabia" to the wide oceans traversed as if a mere brook, they come to see her.

With growing anguish, he revisits the clues.

One of the three contains her "heavenly picture". Is it lead? No, it can't be, it would be damnable to think such a debased thought.

Sinful, too, the notion she could be set in silver which is ten times less valuable than gold. "Never so rich a gem was set in worse than gold", he declares.

With growing intensity, Morocco grasps at whatever symbolism he can muster, however tenuous, to seal his decision. His mind suddenly fixes on the image of a British coin he's seen with the figure of an angel on it stamped in gold. Impulsively comparing the coin's inanimate engraving to the greater value of the very real "angel in a golden bed" within his grasp, he chooses gold, declaring he will take his chances.

Portia, secretly relieved at the outcome, confidently, and somewhat provocatively, hands him the key, declaring, disingenuously, that if her picture is there (she knows it is not) she is his.

Morocco, opens the golden casket, revealing to his shock a skull with a scroll in its eye. The image repulses him, eliciting an angry expletive. He proceeds to read what is written: a cleverly-worded rhyme enlightening him that "all that glitters is not gold", that gold's outward attraction is shallow, and if he were a man of youthful vigour but endowed with more maturity and wisdom, he wouldn't need to learn this lesson here – so, goodbye, you've lost your suit.

With remorse and ill-concealed resentment Morocco declares his despair. He rapidly bids Portia farewell, admitting the humiliation of his loss prevents him from prolonged goodbyes. Snapping to his slaves and servants, he and his entourage abruptly depart.

Portia, in a sudden moment of brutal candour, drops her veneer of high-minded gentility and bids him good riddance, revealing her contempt for his race and hoping that "all of his complexion" will make the same choice as he.

Exeunt.

2.8

An army barracks.

Enter SALARIO and SOLANIO.

Salario and Solanio enter into an animated conversation. Salario informs his partner that he saw Bassanio and Gratiano aboard ship and under sail, but is sure Lorenzo was not with them. Solanio, contemptuously replies that "the villain Jew", as he terms Shylock, has discovered his daughter's absence and treachery and has enlisted intervention by the General who accompanied him to search for her on Bassanio's ship.

Salario salaciously fills out the picture, relating that the General arrived too late to make the inspection since the ship was already under sail, but, while there, was informed that Jessica, the object of his search, was seen in amorous embrace with Lorenzo in a gondola, and Antonio confirmed to the General that she was not hidden aboard his ship.

Solanio, now exhibiting the crude bigotry reminiscent of Gratiano, calls Shylock a "Jew dog" and ridicules his hysteria in the streets at the discovery of Jessica's elopement with the Christian, Lorenzo, and her theft of his ducats and jewels. Cruelly mocking Shylock's distress, he relates with unsuppressed glee that he's never heard an outburst "...so confused, so strange, outrageous, and so variable" in public. A rage wildly vacillating between his daughter's flight, the loss of his ducats, the loss of his jewels, her elopement with a Christian, and his demand that the authorities find her and visit justice upon her for thievery. Salario chimes in with equal delight that all the boys in Venice follow Shylock through the streets mocking him, echoing his cries for "'his stones, his daughter, and his ducats!'"

The implication of Shylock's emotional volatility suddenly registers with Solanio who ominously connects it with Antonio's contract. He anxiously expresses hope that Antonio repay his loan in time lest he pay the price of Shylock's wrath.

Salario concurs, acknowledging Solanio's point to be a good one, and further darkens the picture by relating a conversation he had the day before with a Frenchman who told him that a Venetian vessel heavily laden with cargo had recently been wrecked in the English Channel. He immediately thought of Antonio when he heard this and wished to himself that the ship was not his. Solanio advises Salario to tell Antonio what he's heard, but to break it to him gently lest he be distraught at the news.

Salario muses that Antonio is the kindest, gentlest man in the world. He describes appreciatively how he saw him bid farewell to Bassanio who, affectionately, promised to finish his business as fast as he could in order to hurry back. To which Antonio objected, telling him not to do so, not to do careless work for his sake, and to see his business through to the end. As for the Jew's contract, he told him selflessly not to let it interfere with his work or deflect his attention from the pursuit of love and courtship and how to win his beloved, Portia. At this, Salario relates with studied innocence, Antonio was suddenly overcome with deep emotion, and turned away his face as he wept putting his hand behind him to grasp Bassanio's with deep affection. Then they parted.

Solanio, in a moment of unguarded candour, alludes to what none of their circle dares speak outright, that Antonio bears an unusually deep, and possibly suspect, affection for his comrade Bassanio; that, in fact, he only loves life, itself, because of him. But having trod so close to dangerous ground, Solanio rights himself and abruptly retreats to more prosaic and friendly pursuits, advocating that they seek out Antonio and lift his spirits with some "delight or other".

Salario, readily agrees they should do it!

Exeunt.

[2.8a – insert]

Haifa Port

The scene is Haifa Port, a bustling centre of shipping and British naval activity. On a set of stages adjacent to the harbour a Scots Guard band dressed in formal kilt and military paraphernalia are in concert celebrating the wedding of a British mandatory official. A procession of wedding guests enter dressed to the nines in high-toned attire humorously out of place in a Middle Eastern setting.

Shylock and a compatriot are seen emerging from a black "sherut" (taxi limousine) amidst the bustle of the port. He has come on business, which is his constant preoccupation, but now finds himself surrounded by an unfolding drama he never anticipated. A refugee ship is approaching the port with survivors of Hitler's carnage seeking refuge in Palestine.

British vessels and forces are quickly arrayed blocking their entry. The resulting commotion momentarily diverts the attention of the band, their performance disintegrating in disarray. A wave of disquiet passes through the assembled guests. Abruptly, order is restored by the bandleader as the gathered dignitaries regain their composure and continue their ceremonial progression.

Demonstrators rapidly gather attempting to pressure and harass British forces to allow their brethren entry. A state of chaos soon engulfs the port with the hardier asylum seekers jumping ship in desperate effort to evade the British blockade, forcing naval units to fish them out of the water alive or dead.

A group of refugees, including women with children in tow, have managed to circumvent the first echelon of British patrols and are now being surrounded by reinforcements forcefully taking them in hand for return to their ship and transport to internment camps on Cyprus. A harried young woman being manhandled by a British soldier violently turns and spits in his face.

Shylock, who for most of his life has avoided the political turmoil surrounding him, is now beset by a reality he cannot ignore. Suddenly, out of the crowd being corralled by British forces emerges, apparition-like, the same little "Jessica" of his dream. She advances ghost-like towards him, unaffected by the chaos around her, her arms outstretched in supplication to her father.

Shylock, whose life has been built around a rigid system of personal and religious disciplines and "survival mechanisms" since the loss of his wife, suddenly shatters. He frantically spreads his arms to receive the child, unable to advance towards her, as in his dream. The little girl, real or imagined, turns her head towards him as she is suddenly engulfed by the chaotic crowd being moved violently back to the ship.

Shylock, left frozen alone centre stage as the violence swirls away from him, sinks to his knees, hands grasping his head, emitting a horrific silent scream captured in large projection on the screen upstage. Blackout. The band plays on.

2.9

Belmont House Banqueting Hall.

Enter NERISSA and a servant.

Nerissa hurriedly enters with a servant ordering her to quickly draw straight the curtain concealing the caskets as the next suitor, the Prince of Arragon, having taken his oath, is about to enter to make his choice.

Flourish cornets. Enter the Prince of ARRAGON, his train, and PORTIA.

Finding the process increasingly tedious, Portia dispenses with the grand formalities and directly proposes to Arragon the terms of the venture: "There are the caskets, Prince, if you choose the one which holds my image, we will be wed immediately; if not, you must leave forthwith and without further ado."

Arragon, with a thick Spanish accent accentuated by a Hapsburg lip, reiterates, with some misgiving, the terms of the contract as he understands them. First, never reveal to anyone which casket he chose. Second, if he chooses the wrong box, never again propose marriage to anyone in his lifetime. Third, if he fails in his quest, to immediately leave and be gone.

Portia declares sardonically, and with growing tedium, much to the amusement of the gathered guests, that everyone who comes to compete for her "worthless self" must play by these rules.

Arragon declares himself ready, and methodically proceeds to analyse his choices, hoping that luck will grant him his heart's desire: gold, silver, and base lead; "Who chooseth me must give and hazard all he hath."

He first declares dismissively regarding lead, that it would have to be more beautiful before he'd risk anything for it.

His attention then turns to the golden chest: "Who chooseth me shall gain what many men desire."

"Ah! Let's see", he ponders. "What many men desire" … That "many" may mean the foolish vulgarity of popular taste enticed by outward shows devoid of deeper meaning – seduced by only what meets the eye. Like the martlet bird, which builds its nests on outer walls, even in the face of adverse conditions, too many are concerned only with outward appearance. "I will not choose what many men desire", lest I "jump with common spirits and rank me with the barbarous multitudes".

Thus, his prolonged analysis turns once again to the silver casket. He considers once more its message: "Who chooseth me shall get as much as he deserves."

Enamoured by what he sees as the profundity of this maxim, Arragon goes off, verbosely, on a tangent. Forgetting the purpose of the task before him, he waxes philosophical on the implications of the casket's quotation.

The proposition is well said he muses, for all honours should be truly deserved. Let no one presume a status undeserved by accomplishment. If only all wealth, status, and positions were achieved by merit rather than corruption, and honour was clearly the product of merit alone. Thus, as the Bible says, "the last will be first and the first last", the peasant would gain nobility and the nobleman learn humility. "How many be commanded that command! How much low peasantry would then be gleaned from the true seed of honour! And how much honour picked from the chaff and ruin of the times to be new varnished!"

Abruptly, Arragon's attention abandons his bloviating and returns to the task at hand. "Who chooseth me shall get as much as he deserves", he considers once again. Concluding that he, indeed, is deserving, he demands the key for silver to instantly unlock his fortune.

Arragon opens the silver casket.

Observing the result – which she already knew beforehand – Portia, with amusement and subtle contempt, observes dryly that the Spanish prince expended too much thought for the "prize" obtained.

Arragon, in disbelief, peers into the box where the picture of a "blinking idiot" with a scroll in hand stares up at him. Flummoxed by the result and still not cognisant of its meaning, he remarks dumbly he will read the scroll – but how unlike Portia is the image contained there! Stifled laughter spreads through the crowd. With growing realisation and distress, Arragon whines that this outcome wasn't what he'd hoped for at all or what he deserves.

"'Who chooseth me shall have as much as he deserves!' Did I deserve no more than a fool's head? Is that my prize? Are my deserts no better?" he moans.

Portia responds patronisingly that judgment and offense are two different functions. The silver casket has performed the first, and she will refrain from further comment to avoid the second!

Arragon, still befuddled by his misfortune, persists in reading the cryptic message held by the fool exposing how silver can be deceptive: the box and its judgment have been tested seven times by fire and never proven wrong; only the infallible can stand its test; those that kiss at shadows only achieve the shadow of happiness; there are fools alive who are "silvered o'er" – and so was this; take whatever wife you will, you will always have a fool's head hanging over you. "So, be gone." And quickly, too.

Defeated, Arragon morosely acknowledges that the longer he stays, the more fool he appears. Self-pityingly, he laments that he came to woo Portia bearing one fool's head, and now he leaves with two! Mustering what gallantry he has left, he bids Portia a sweet farewell, reaffirming his oath, determined to accept his anger and humiliation with forbearance.

Exeunt ARRAGON and his train.

Portia, grown weary of the travesty unfolding before her, compares the men pursuing her to moths repeatedly burned by the flame of her caskets. What a bunch of fools she cries, who only have the "wisdom" to lose.

Nerissa, consoles her with an ancient proverb she believes may be true: "destiny determines when you'll hang and when you'll wed!"

Resigned, Portia orders her to draw the curtain.

Enter MESSENGER.

Suddenly, a messenger arrives asking for the lady of the house, bearing news that a young Venetian has arrived at her gate announcing the imminent arrival of his master, who not only sends courteous and attractive greetings but also very expensive gifts, the likes of which he has never seen, nor a more attractive candidate for her love. A lovely day in spring never came so enticingly as the forerunner of a rich summer, as this servant before his master.

Portia's interest, now suddenly aroused, cuts off the messenger's promotion of the mystery candidate with the wry repost that she's half afraid the man may be one of his relatives he touts him so extravagantly! She abruptly beckons Nerissa to come along with her, for she longs to see this polished arrival Cupid has sent her.

Nerissa declares her hope that the surprise is Bassanio.

Exeunt.

[2.9a – insert]

Jerusalem, Central Bus Station.

Shylock emerges once again from a "sherut" on his return to Jerusalem. Still dazed and disoriented by his experience on the Haifa docks, he is helped from the vehicle by his business associate who offers to guide him home. Shylock waves him off and stumbles into the street, navigating his way through anonymous throngs going about their business unaffected by him.

The normal flow of the crowd is physically transformed, through choreography, sound effects and lighting, reflecting Shylock's profound and growing disorientation. A monstrous dreamscape emerges populated by the denizens of a living Hell, reflecting, in his tormented mind, the crises afflicting Mandatory Palestine and his personal agonies.

These grotesques, initially oblivious to Shylock's presence in their underworld, start to take notice of him. With growing rancour, they torment him as he passes through them with malevolent stares and threatening violence. Malicious children appear, plaguing him like an inescapable swarm, with stinging taunts and hostile provocations. Groups of British soldiers – the recognisable figures of Gratiano, Solanio and Salario among them – gesticulate mockingly and obscenely; masquers revel before him bedevilling him with obscenities and hideous faces.

He passes clandestine tête–à–têtes of Nazi agents and Fedayeen first seen at Portia's soirée. They blankly fix their gaze upon him; an Arab of their party mimes the slitting of his throat. All about him projection screens come alive like firing synapses graphically depicting violent newspaper headlines and newsreel footage of brutality – the Hebron and Hadassah hospital massacres, Fedayeen attacks on kibbutzim, violent Irgun and Stern gang reprisals, the retaliatory lynching by Irgun of three British soldiers. Shylock tries frantically to escape these ghouls and make his way to refuge, but none can be found.

His initial disgust at the lowlife debauchery of occupation forces and the incitement of his persecutors (Antonio, Gratiano, et al.), escalates into horror at the image, once again, of refugees beset by British shore-patrols, and CID murders of Jewish dissidents, portrayed in this netherworld of nightmare by the assassination of extremist resistance leader, Avram Stern, by Gratiano on a Tel Aviv street.

The image of a profligate Jessica, pet monkey on her shoulder, appears before him, wantonly flaunting her monies stolen from him now supporting a new lifestyle of immodest dress and manners. Her image cuts Shylock to the quick in a confusion of rage, guilt, and remorse. He tries desperately to exorcise the spectre, tormentedly reciting the prayer for the dead, the Kaddish (Yit'gadal v'yit'kadash sh'mei raba... May His great Name grow exalted and sanctified...) for a daughter lost to him, but to no avail. The demon Jessica laughs with contempt in his face before receding into darkness, replaced by the next terror to come.

Out of this cauldron of horror, the little girl in Haifa port suddenly emerges, evoking the image of his own Jessica in childhood. Her angelic innocence, juxtaposed to her betrayal and flight, finally sends Shylock over the edge. Numb with shock, rage, and grief, now beyond all sense of proportion, he blindly stumbles, sobbing, to his door.

ACT THREE

3.1

A street in the Old City.

Enter SOLANIO and SALARIO.

Solanio and Salario, much enmeshed in the plotting surrounding Antonio and Lorenzo, enter into intense conversation over the state of affairs. Solanio enquires what the news is in the Rialto, to which Salario replies that rumours are rife that a ship of Antonio's laden with rich cargo has been wrecked on the Goodwin Sands, a very dangerous and deadly shoal in the English Channel where many unfortunate crafts lie buried – if stories be true.

Solanio, with ostentatiously exaggerated compassion, expresses hope that such stories are as big a lie as the claim by the town gossip of her tearful grief at the death of her third husband! But he begins to confirm it is true – only to suddenly get hung-up mid-sentence by a search for the appropriate honorific by which to title and praise Antonio, "the good", "the honest..."

Impatiently interrupting him, Salario retorts that he should get to the point!

Solanio, dropping his histrionics, declares with dramatic understatement that Antonio's ship is lost!

Salario replies hoping that will be the full extent of his losses!

Solanio, suddenly catching sight of Shylock in the street stumbling in their direction, cuts off discussion with an "Amen", contemptuously alluding to the approaching threat of the devil in "the likeness of a Jew", about to violate his prayers.

Enter SHYLOCK.

With subtle mockery he greets Shylock and inquires after the merchants in the Rialto.

Shylock, having none of their banter confronts and accuses them. They knew, he charges them with quivering rage – no one knew better than they of his daughter's plans to flee.

With cruel mockery, Salario, indeed, takes credit for complicity in Jessica's escape declaring that he even knows the tailor who created the disguise in which she ran off!

Solanio further chimes in that Shylock, himself, must have known it was time for her to leave the nest, and that it is altogether natural for a child to do so.

Unmollified, Shylock declares his daughter will be damned for it! To which Solanio counters contemptuously, that will be certain, if the Devil is the judge!

Shylock, undeterred, declares his rage that his own flesh and blood rebels against him, to which Solanio, playing crudely on the double entendre of rebelling flesh as a euphemism for an erection, mocks the idea that a man of his age could even have one.

Shylock, ensconced in rage and oblivious to the point of Solanio's jibes, makes it clear he means his daughter is his "flesh and blood." Not to be outdone, Salario chimes in with further disparagement, declaring there is greater difference between Shylock's flesh and that of his daughter than between "jet and ivory" or between "red wine and rhenish." He then glibly dismisses the subject, enquiring as to whether Shylock is privy to any news regarding the fate of Antonio's ships at sea.

Shylock, apparently aware of Antonio's losses, redirects his rage. He bemoans his deal with Antonio as "another bad match" made with "a bankrupt, a prodigal who dare scarce show his head on the Rialto, a beggar that was used to come so smug upon the mart".

Shylock's accumulated resentments for past indignities at Antonio's hands well up in him, and for the first time take on a menacing air of vengeance. "Let him look to his bond", he declares. "He was wont to call me usurer; let him look to his bond. He was wont to lend money for a Christian courtesy; let him look to his bond."

Salario, taken aback by Shylock's sudden vindictiveness, sounds out his intentions, expressing his certainty that Shylock would never really take Antonio's flesh, for "what's that good for?" To which Shylock, in a sudden flash of rage reflecting a lifetime of degradation and abuse, made the more acute by his daughter's betrayal in collaboration with his persecutors, holds forth with the full depth and brunt of his injury and need for retribution. If nothing else taking Antonio's flesh will "feed (his) revenge" he maniacally weeps, for Antonio has "disgraced" him publicly, and cost him a fortune financially. He's laughed at his losses and ridiculed his hard-earned profits, disgraced his people, compromised his business, alienated his friends, and provoked his enemies — and all because he is a Jew!

In a wave of despair and pain, Shylock now confronts the world, and himself, with the existential question at the base of his suffering: "Hath not a Jew eyes?!!"

Do Jews not have the same bodies as Christians, he demands? Are they not fed with the same food, injured with the same weapons, sickened by the same diseases, and healed by the same means as they are? Are they not as responsive to the warmth and cold of the seasons as a Christian is?

And if Jews bleed, laugh, and die as Christians do, why when they are wronged shall they not revenge as Christians do, as well? Have they not all the dimensions of a man in every aspect – all the "senses, affections, passions" that are part of a human being?

The rage long repressed by Shylock, the victim, now erupts at Antonio his persecutor: if a Jew wrongs a Christian what will he suffer? Revenge! And if a Jew is wronged by a Christian, what should be his response? Why, revenge, by Christian example! In this explosive moment Shylock confronts Antonio with a compelling claim for equality through the logic of retribution. What is more, Shylock vows, not only will he learn from Christian example, he will "better the instruction!"

Thus, in a moment of profound emotional and moral transformation, Shylock rejects a lifetime of degradation and submission at the hands of the Christian world. Proclaiming the question, "Hath not a Jew eyes?", not as an ineffectual plea for mercy, but as a brief for revenge!

Enter a MAN from Antonio.

Shylock's speech is suddenly broken by the arrival of a servant of Antonio's requesting the presence of Solanio and Salario. Salario declares that they, in fact, have been searching "up and down" for him.

Enter TUBAL.

At which point Tubal, a friend and business associate of Shylock's, appears on the scene, eliciting from Solanio the further antisemitic slight: "Here comes another of the tribe. A third cannot be matched unless the devil himself turn Jew".

Exeunt SOLANIO, SALARIO, and SERVANT.

Shylock, drained and unstable in the wake of his emotional outburst, finds some solace in the sight of his old friend, whom he greets with an observably weak composure. He enquires of developments in Genoa and the whereabouts of his daughter.

Tubal replies that he often came to places where he "heard of her" but could not find her.

Shylock, beside himself with grief and confusion, redirects yet again the focus of his grief, now bemoaning the material loss of his jewels – a diamond costing two thousand ducats purchased in Frankfurt and other gems. He pathetically obsesses on the loss declaring with self-pity that the "curse" of being a Jew was never fully felt by him until now.

Suddenly, the rage returns as Shylock erratically directs his ire against Jessica and her betrayal resentfully wishing her "dead" at his feet with "the jewel in her ear" and laid in her coffin with the stolen ducats. Overwhelmed with frustration and despair at the failure to find Jessica, Shylock retreats to a litany of remorse and self-pity, lamenting his losses and the monies further lost in effort to regain them – but above all bemoaning, "no satisfaction, no revenge". Nor, he cries, does bad luck seek anyone but him, no suffering and no tears are other than his own.

Tubal tries to calm him, placing his arm around Shylock's shoulder and guiding him out of the view of the street, where he has aroused growing attention from passers-by to a quiet bench in a nearby garden. In effort to console him, Tubal remarks, obliquely, that based on rumours he's heard in Genoa, Shylock is not the only one now suffering "ill-luck".

Immediately, taking his meaning to be Antonio, Shylock – in a continuing state of mania – breaks off his self-pity, his attention now suddenly sparked in a new direction. Sputtering, "What, what, what? Ill luck, ill luck?", his thoughts are now alive with schadenfreude at the expense of his nemesis, Antonio.

Tubal calmly confirms that Antonio lost a ship sailing from Tripoli.

Shylock, beside himself with satisfaction, thanks God and demands confirmation the story is true.

Tubal replies that he spoke with sailors who had escaped the wreck itself.

Suddenly elated, Shylock profusely thanks Tubal for the good news heard in Genoa which now dominates his state of mind.

Tubal, however, feels compelled to break his celebration with news of a more sobering nature.

He's also heard in Genoa that Jessica spent eighty ducats in one night of excess.

Shylock is stricken, declaring the news to be like a dagger in him, lamenting he will never see his gold again, mindlessly repeating the unbelievable figure of "fourscore ducats at a sitting", now irretrievably lost.

Tubal further reveals that he came to Genoa in the company of a variety of other creditors of Antonio's who "swear" he must go bankrupt.

Seamlessly grasping the opportunity this affords for revenge, Shylock coldly affirms his pleasure at the news of Antonio's misfortune and vows to "plague" and "torture him" with it.

Tubal, in a strange moment of seeming insensitivity pours further oil on the fire, telling Shylock the emotionally devastating news that one of the creditors showed him a ring he had purchased from Jessica for a monkey!

Shylock is suddenly transfixed and shattered. On the brink of collapse, Shylock implores Tubal to stop torturing him. The ring in question was a turquoise given to him by Leah before they were married, embodying a past life of love, tenderness, humanity, and a cherished daughter now lost to him. In a devastating moment of grief and vulnerability Shylock reveals emotionally that despite his all too frequent rage and resentments, the most valuable jewel lost to him is, in fact, his daughter Jessica, alienated now beyond redemption. He sobs uncontrollably, oblivious to all else around him, declaring chaotically in the throes of his passion that he "would not have given (the ring) for a wilderness of monkeys."

Tubal, in service to an agenda yet not clear, brings the devastated Shylock back to the subject of Antonio's fall, as if it in some way compensates for Shylock's suffering – "But Antonio is certainly undone."

Shylock, emotionally exhausted, weakly mutters his assent and through remaining tears instructs Tubal to engage a police officer two weeks in advance to arrest Antonio. Should he forfeit the loan he will immediately have Antonio's heart. In a state of growing disorientation and confusion, Shylock anticipates the competitive advantages that will accrue from Antonio's elimination.

Carefully observing Shylock's condition and reactions, Tubal now takes his friend in hand purposefully and firmly guides him from the scene. The motivation for his studied provocations piquing Shylock's rage now become apparent as Tubal furtively acknowledges the presence nearby of our three young friends from the Irgun, "innocently" enjoying an ice-cream in the park on a delightful, sunny day in Jerusalem.

Exeunt severally.

3.2

Belmont House Garden

Enter BASSANIO, PORTIA, GRATIANO, NERISSA, and all their trains, including a SINGER.

Portia's encounter with her new Venetian suitor has gone well it seems, for we now find her in an observably solicitous mood as she entertains her new guest. Her change of heart is palpable and in sharp contrast to the cynicism shown to his predecessors. A countertenor, singing *Amarili, mia bella* romantically croons in the background, the mood languid and enticing. Amidst these atmospherics Portia addresses Bassanio in what can only be described as growing enamourment and confusion – her normal control and authority observably fraying at his sight. Trying the while to maintain her composure, Portia openly expresses hope he might wait a day or two before proceeding with the challenge, admitting she would hate to lose his company if he chose wrongly.

Catching herself in this moment of candour, Portia quickly (and unconvincingly) asserts that her feelings are not "love" as such, but…something tells her that she wouldn't want to lose him, and "hate" certainly wouldn't prompt her to think that way!

Getting progressively more flustered, Portia further clarifies that in case Bassanio doesn't understand her clearly, and because a young woman has no other means of expressing her desires, she'd like Bassanio to stay a month or two before taking the test! She could help him make the right choice she muses, in a state of growing fantasy and excitement, but then again, no, she catches herself … that would be impossible, a violation of her oath, so she'll never tell – but then Bassanio might fail the test and lose her which would make her wish she had sinned and violated her oath…!

Portia's emotional agitation reigns supreme as she is suddenly smitten by Bassanio's eyes! Her feelings now find voice without inhibition: his gaze has divided her in two; one half is already his, the other half – which should be hers – his also. So, all is his! But in these terrible times, she mourns, people are barred from their own possessions; thus, she laments, while his, not his!

With sudden stoicism she breaks off her reveries. If it is her fate to lose him, then do it now – let Fortune be damned for the outcome not her! Placing herself at the mercy of Fate, Portia candidly admits she has spoken too long, her aim to draw out the time with Bassanio and delay the moment of truth.

Bassanio also pleads to proceed immediately claiming that life in such uncertainty is torturous, as if upon the rack.

Portia, with an intuition that grasps more than she immediately realises, picks up on Bassanio's allusion to "the rack", challenging him to confess what "treason" mixed with his love justifies such punishment?

Bassanio, ever the charmer – as his "friend" Antonio well knows – deflects Portia's probing with agile wit and perfect response: his only fear, he responds, is the "ugly treason of mistrust" that Portia will ever be his; there may as well be intimacy between "snow and fire", as between his love and treason (perish the thought!).

Pursuing the analogy further, part in truth, part in jest, and part defensively, Portia casts doubt on Bassanio's claims reminding him that men under torture will confess anything.

Bassanio, parries by means of a bargain: a promise of "life" from "Portia, the Judge", in exchange for "the truth", from him.

Portia accepts the deal, telling him to "confess and live."

Bassanio breaks off the game declaring, "Confess and love", to be his full "confession", and happily claiming torment a pleasure when the torturer provides the answers for deliverance!

With the growing assurance and irrationality of a gambler convinced of a lucky roll – and aware that if luck doesn't come with money in the bank in addition to more spiritual pursuits there's no point in hanging around – Bassanio demands they proceed straightway to his "fortune and the caskets".

With sudden sobriety Portia tells him to go. She is locked in one of the caskets and if his love is sincere, he'll find her there. Portia orders Nerissa and the others to stand away from him and that music be played while he decides, so that if he loses the end will fade in music like a swan song. And to make the comparison the more poignant, her tears will be the "stream and the watery death bed for him".

But if he wins, what music should be played then? The glorious tribute when loyal subjects bow to a king newly crowned, or the soothing sounds at sunrise of church bells calling a dreaming bridegroom to marriage.

In nervous obsession, Portia narrates the unfolding drama of Bassanio's advance, comparing him to no less than Alcides (Hercules) on a mission to save the princess Hesione given as tribute to a sea-monster. But Bassanio's love for her, she is convinced, is greater than that of Alcides for the Princess.

Managing the excruciating tension of the moment by fully embracing the classical fantasy Portia casts herself as the object of "sacrifice", and her entourage the weeping "Dardanian" wives come to observe the exploits. "Go Hercules", she exclaims. "Live thou, I live. With much, much more dismay I view the fight than thou that makest the fray."

A song whilst BASSANIO comments on the caskets to himself.

Bassanio, from the outset, is suspicious of the glitter and appeal of outward show. He waxes philosophical about "ornament" and its uses to deceive.

Before the courts a corrupt plea can be advanced by a charming voice concealing evil intent. Doesn't religion often justify vice by means of scripture and bless it, concealing iniquity behind a beautiful text? There is no sin too small that can't acquire some outward sign of goodness.

How often do lily-livered cowards lacking in all fortitude posture and display the bearded image of Hercules and Mars – their outward "valour" nothing more than "excrement"?

Beauty, itself, can be purchased "by weight" as make-up and miraculously change a woman's appearance, but its effects are not convincing; those that use it most are least admired.

And "golden locks" that bounce so playfully and provocatively in the breeze are often the bequest of a head now in the grave! So, ornament is misleading, like a treacherous shore to dangerous seas, or a beautiful scarf concealing an exotic and dangerous Indian woman.

Simply put, ornament is deceptive, and these days is widely used to fool even the wisest.

So, glittering gold which Midas couldn't eat, I'll have none of your box.

Nor will I choose pale silver, the stuff of which coins are made, and common commerce conducted between men.

I will choose you, unimpressive lead, even though you appear more threatening than promising, your pallor touches me more than I can say. So, here is my choice! May joy be the result!

Portia, now beside herself, knows Bassanio has made the right choice. In her ecstasy she feels all other emotions – thoughts of doubt, despair, fear, and jealousy – disappear to the point that she appeals to love itself for mercy. She pleads for love to "be moderate", to put aside its extremes, rein-in its joys, and diminish its abundance. Make her love less, she implores, lest overwhelmed by her passion she becomes ill.

Bassanio opens the lead casket to find a picture of Portia. He is transfixed by the likeness of the portrait to life. What godlike artist could have created such eyes that seem to move, such parted lips separated by sweet breath, hair so fine in texture like a spider's web to trap the hearts of men more swiftly than "gnats in cobwebs?"

But the eyes, he exclaims, how could the artist have finished one so exquisitely and still had the power to finish the other?! Yet, I fail to do the picture justice – wonderful as it is, it is just a "shadow" of the real Portia. He then finds the scroll, which, he remarks, will determine his "fate."

The scroll in verse declares that by not choosing by outward show alone, you have had the best luck. Since fortune is yours, be satisfied with it and seek nothing else. If you agree and are pleased with this, hold your good luck for your happiness, and "turn to where your lady is and claim her with a loving kiss".

Bassanio stands in a daze, still not convinced of his good fortune. He turns to Portia, praises the scroll's contents, and hesitantly asks her leave to offer himself with a kiss, as the scroll instructs. Bassanio declares he still can't believe his luck – it's as if he's won a competition, is dazzled with excitement thinking he's done well, and despite hearing the cheers of the crowd is still unsure that the praise is really his. And he will remain so three times over until victory is confirmed, signed, and ratified by her.

In a striking transformation, Portia, the general's daughter, self-assured and liberated, melts in the heat of love. She expresses a sudden humility, even self-deprecation, declaring to Bassanio that she stands before him without pretence – what he sees is what she is. Though she is satisfied with herself for herself alone, for him she would wish herself twenty times better than she is – more beautiful a thousand times, and richer by ten thousand – to be more highly prized by him. That "I might in virtue, beauties, livings, friends exceed account." Suddenly, all façade and defence fall away revealing a young woman, who, by her own account, is "an unlessoned girl, unschooled, unpractised." But one who is not too old or too ignorant to learn. And in ultimate submission (or seduction as the case may be), Portia declares her joy that her "gentle spirit" now is Bassanio's – "her lord, her governor, her king" – to direct as he wishes. She and all she possesses are now his. Moments ago, she was mistress of this magnificent estate, commander of her servants, sovereign over herself. But as of this moment – house, servants, and she, herself – are all his, conveyed by her ring, which if he leaves, loses, or gives away will mean the destruction of their love and justify her enmity towards him.

(Gives BASSANIO a ring)

Bassanio, overwhelmed, replies to Portia that all words have left him, only his emotions coursing in the blood of his veins speaks to her now. And there is such a wild jumble of emotions as attend the adulation of a crowd after a charismatic speech by a beloved prince, where every feeling mixed together turns wildly into nothing but joy, spoken or unspoken. And Bassanio vows that the day this ring leaves his finger is the day he dies. You can be sure he is dead if you see him without it!

Nerissa now heartily congratulates the couple as does Gratiano, who in a display of gushing comradery requests that when Bassanio is married he wishes to be married too.

Bassanio enthusiastically agrees provided Gratiano can find a wife in time.

Eager to further ingratiate himself to his establishment "buddy" and solidify a position in his inner circle, Gratiano thanks Bassanio for advancing his own marital prospects, as well. Comparing himself with Bassanio's quest for Portia, Gratiano boasts that he too has been "on the prowl" and just as Bassanio "saw the mistress" he "saw the maid". "You loved, I loved." And he's no more inclined to delay than Bassanio whose fate hung on the caskets and, as it happens, so did his. After strenuously wooing her with oaths of love until his mouth ran dry, he finally received Nerissa's promise – if it remains true – that she would give him her love if Bassanio and Portia were wed.

Portia, who has never been impressed by Gratiano, is momentarily taken aback by the romantic adventures of her servant, Nerissa, under her very nose. She sceptically enquires of Nerissa if Gratiano's statement is true.

Nerissa, a bit on the desperate side and appreciative of the attentions of even a down-market character like Gratiano, says that it is if it's alright with her.

Bassanio, knowing the rougher side of Gratiano, enquires in the interests of propriety whether what he says is in good faith.

Gratiano assures him that it is, to which Bassanio, cutting off further discussion, declares they'd be "honoured" to have them.

Gratiano, flying high in a sudden flush of machismo, proposes to Nerissa that they bet their friends a thousand ducats that they'll have a son first.

Nerissa, shocked by the suggestion, asks sceptically if he means to "stake down" the money now.

Gratiano, suddenly reverting to his true crudity, replies jocularly (with a play on words of the term "stake" – slang for penis) that they'll never win the bet if he "stake(s) down!" Gratiano's sexual chauvinism is followed hard upon by his antisemitism as he announces the arrival of "Lorenzo and his 'infidel' (Jessica) … and my old Venetian friend Salerio".

Enter LORENZO, JESSICA, and SALARIO, a messenger from Venice.

Bassanio welcomes Lorenzo and Salario to the house – as if his newly acquired status empowers him to. But, immediately catching his presumption, he asks permission of Portia, with studied humility, if he might welcome his old comrades as guests.

Portia accommodatingly agrees, extending her warm welcome too.

Lorenzo replies that, actually, he didn't come to see Bassanio, but ran into Salario who begged him so intensely to come along that he couldn't refuse.

Salario confirms that he did so for good reason – Signor Antonio recommends him to you.

(Gives BASSANIO a letter.)

Before reading the letter, Bassanio enquires how his friend is faring. Salario replies that he's not physically ill but extremely distressed emotionally. His letter will give the details.

BASSANIO opens the letter and reads.

Gratiano, in emulation of his "role-model" Bassanio, exercises his own faux-authority over wife-to-be Nerissa ordering her to extend hospitality to Jessica – whom he had derisively referred to as an "infidel" a few minutes earlier – as if she were now a welcome stranger. Turning to Salario he greets him magnanimously with an overly hearty hand and enquires about developments in Venice, disingenuously asking after "that royal merchant, good Antonio?" (who he knows is now in peril). Gratiano declares boastfully that he is sure he'll be pleased with their accomplishments. Like Jason, "we have won the fleece!".

Salario caustically replies with a "play on words" (conflating "fleece" and "fleets") that he wishes they had won the "fleece" he's just lost.

Portia watches with growing concern as the blood drains from Bassanio's cheeks and concludes there must be something dreadfully wrong to change the visage of a man of his fortitude so much. It could only be the death of a dear friend – but no, is the news getting worse?! She begs Bassanio, since she is now his "other half", to let her bear with him half the burdens the letter contains.

Bassanio is horrified by what he has just read calling the letter some of the most terrible words ever put to paper. Remorsefully, he makes confession to his "sweet Portia". When first he gave her his love, he told her forthrightly and honestly that all the wealth he had ran in his veins. He was a gentleman but without means. And yet even that was an exaggeration for he, in truth, was less than nothing. He should have told her then that what means he did have were borrowed from a dear friend who in turn had borrowed from his deadly enemy on his behalf.

Bassanio, displays the letter comparing it to the body of his friend and declaring dramatically "every word in it" to be "a gaping wound, issuing life blood". In disbelief, Bassanio demands confirmation from Salario that all Antonio's ships have been lost – not one success from Tripoli, from Mexico and England to Lisbon, Barbary, and India? Not one ship avoided the devastation of merchant-wrecking rocks?!

Salario confirms not one has survived, and in any event even if Antonio had enough money now to pay the Jew, he wouldn't accept it. Never had he seen a being in human form so intent on destroying a man. He's petitioning the General day and night and indicting the state for denial of freedom of trade "if they deny him justice". "Twenty merchants, the General himself" and the nobility have all sought to convince him. But none can dissuade him from the bitter claim "of forfeiture, of justice, and his bond".

Jessica, who has been listening all the while, further confirms that when she lived with Shylock, she "heard him swear" to his compatriots, Tubal and Chus, "that he would rather have Antonio's flesh than twenty times the … sum that he did owe him", and unless the law and the state intercede, Antonio's fate will be a hard one.

Portia asks Bassanio if it is his dear friend that is in such trouble.

Bassanio confirms it is so, further commending him as "the dearest friend to me, the kindest man", tirelessly courteous and possessed of the "ancient Roman honour" more than any in Italy.

Portia asks how much he owes the Jew.

Bassanio replies that on his account three thousand ducats.

Surprised by what to her seems a paltry sum Portia tells Bassanio to pay him six thousand ducats to terminate the debt. In fact, she will double the six thousand and then treble it before she would let a friend of such virtue "lose a hair through Bassanio's fault".

Portia's authority now returns. She tells Bassanio to wed her forthwith and then proceed immediately to Venice to his friend, for he will never be at peace beside her until this crisis is resolved. She promises Bassanio enough gold to repay the debt "twenty times over". And when it is paid return here with your friend. Meanwhile, she declares, she and Nerissa will live chastely as "maids and widows". But "come away", she hurries him, since he will be leaving her the same day of their wedding. Cheerfully welcome your friends. "Since you are dear bought, I will love you dear." But first, Portia asks to see the letter from his friend.

Bassanio reads the letter, which relates that Antonio's ships have all been lost, his creditors are increasingly hostile, his money is almost gone, and the loan from the Jew is forfeit. Since paying the collateral of a pound of flesh will certainly mean his death, all debts between them will be cleared if he could see him when he dies. In any event, do what you feel, if your feelings don't move you to come, disregard the letter.

Portia is deeply and innocently moved by Antonio's plea (not realising the hidden passion behind it) and tells her darling Bassanio to drop everything and go to his friend straight away. Bassanio declares that since he has her permission to leave, he will make all haste and will not even take the time to sleep until he returns to her.

Exeunt.

3.3

A street in Jerusalem.

Enter SHYLOCK, SOLANIO, ANTONIO, and the jailer.

Antonio, accompanied by Solanio, is being allowed a break from his cell and a walk through the streets by the jailer. Shylock, still in a fit of rage, tags along obsessively badgering him and the jailer along the way – his stream of abuse as much an internal narrative as an effort to communicate with either of them. Becoming increasingly unhinged he admonishes the jailer to watch Antonio carefully (as if he were a danger) for the dubious reason that he lent money without charging interest.

Antonio, in desperation, tries to talk reason to him.

His overture is immediately rebuffed by Shylock obsessively demanding his "bond". He won't hear objection to his "bond" – he's sworn an oath that he'll have it. Shylock's accumulated resentments flood to the surface and intermix with his demands. He confronts Antonio with his past abuses and reminds him that he called him a "dog" without cause – threatening that if he's a dog he should fear his fangs! He is sure the General will give him "justice." He then admonishes the jailer for being so foolish as to grant Antonio's request to leave his cell.

Antonio begs him listen.

Shylock fanatically resumes demands for his "bond". He won't hear Antonio speak. He wants his "bond" and he'll hear no more! His resentments towards Christian society and its abuses well up in him. Shylock asserts he won't back down "to shake the head, relent and sigh, and yield" and be made a submissive fool by Christian intruders. Turning his back on Antonio, Shylock, who up 'til then had pursued confrontation with him, now orders him not to follow — he'll have no further talk. "(He'll) have his bond."

Exit SHYLOCK.

Watching Shylock depart, Solanio derisively calls him the most stiff-necked dog that ever kept the company of men.

Antonio, resignedly, tells Solanio to desist from pursuit of Shylock that he'll attempt no more to move him with "bootless prayers". It is now clear to him that Shylock wants him dead, but he persists in the notion that it is because of Shylock's greed — resenting the aid he's given other creditors facing forfeiture — rather than his abuse of Shylock that animates "the Jew's" hatred of him.

Solanio expresses confidence that the General will never allow a judgment to be made against him and enforced.

Antonio thinks otherwise. The General cannot afford to undercut the law. To do so would destroy the confidence that the great diversity of merchants from many lands have in their security here which in turn would seriously damage trade and commerce. But enough! Antonio declares he's lost so much weight worrying about his troubles and losses that he won't have a pound of flesh to satisfy his "bloody creditor" the next day. He bids the jailer continue, praying to God that Bassanio arrives to see him "pay his debt" (and all that implies regarding his devotion to him), and then nothing matters.

Exeunt.

3.4

Belmont House.

Enter PORTIA, NERISSA, LORENZO, JESSICA, and BALTHASAR, a servant of PORTIA'S.

An over-earnest Lorenzo ostentatiously addresses his admiration of Portia for the noble and selfless way she has honoured "true" friendship by allowing Bassanio to go to the aid of Antonio in his moment of need. And if she knew how truly good a man he is, and how devoutly he loves her husband, she would be even prouder of her sacrifice than usual.

Portia casually acknowledges her own virtue by responding with an air of understated humility that she'd never lamented doing good and won't do so now; for men who spend considerable time together, who are soulmates sharing equal feelings of love for each other, must also share similar attributes, natures, and temperaments. This leads her to believe that the two must be very much the same. If this is so, what a meagre price she'd paid to save the image of her soul (so close to Bassanio's and by extension, Antonio's) from such frightful brutality. But, at this, Portia catches herself. Realising her observations are coming too close to self-flattery and bad form, she turns to other matters; giving Lorenzo mastery of Belmont until Bassanio's return. Until then, Portia vows to "live in prayer and contemplation" only in the company of Nerissa. They will reside in a monastery two miles from Belmont. She makes a special plea to Lorenzo not to deny her request to administer Belmont, imposition though it may be, "which my love and some necessity now lays upon you".

Lorenzo devoutly agrees to do all she reasonably desires.

Portia tells him that all the staff have been notified and will look upon him and Jessica as lord and lady of the house in place of Bassanio and herself, and bids him farewell.

Lorenzo wishes her "fair thoughts and happy hours", and Jessica declares, "all hearts content".

Portia thanks them for their good wishes, returns them in kind, and bids a final farewell to Jessica.

Exeunt JESSICA and LORENZO.

Now alone with Balthasar, Portia expresses appreciation for his honesty and faithfulness and, in hope that he will remain so, entrusts him with a letter to be delivered with all possible speed directly to her cousin in Padua, a Doctor Bellario. She instructs him to gather whatever clothes and articles Bellario will give him and bring them straight to the ferry landing that connects to Venice, where she will be waiting for him.

Balthasar pledges to go as fast as possible.

Exit BALTHASAR.

Portia now informs her trusty companion Nerissa she should come along, for she has business to attend to that she hasn't yet told her of, and that they'll see their husbands before they have a chance to miss them.

Nerissa asks if their husbands will see them. To which, Portia, with a sly twinkle in her eye, says, yes, but they'll be dressed in men's clothing and will be taken for "one of the boys". Portia then holds forth satirically on the various imitations of young manhood she'll employ to make the deception complete, claiming puckishly that when they'll be dressed like "young men" she'll bet that she'll be the better looking of the two, sporting her dagger more elegantly, speaking with the changing voice of an adolescent between "man and boy", and replacing her dainty steps with a virile stride. Like a boastful teen she'll tell of fights and fanciful amorous exploits, of "honourable ladies" who died of love for her – after all I couldn't accommodate them all! – then she'll show remorse and wish she hadn't killed them! 20 such petty inventions she'll tell so that everyone will think she left school over a year ago. She knows a thousand such juvenile deceits and will use them!

Nerissa, still in the dark, enquires why they are "turning to men". Portia, facetiously, plays off the "double-entendre", in shock that she should ask a question which could be interpreted by a "dirty mind" as advocating seeking sex from men! But Portia now hurries her along to the coach which is waiting for them where she will explain her plan, for they have twenty miles to cover that day.

Exeunt.

3.5

Belmont House.

Enter LAUNCELET and JESSICA.

Launcelet and Jessica enter in animated conversation. Launcelet, his usual provocative self, expresses concern for Jessica's predicament as Shylock's daughter and likely to be punished for the sins of the father. He avers he's always been straight with her, so now he'll give her the benefit of his opinion: Cheer up, you're *DAMNED!* You have only one hope and a "bastard hope" at that.

Jessica enquires what that hope may be?

Launcelet offers the sage advice that she can hope that her father, Shylock, didn't really father her – that he's not her real father – and she is not "the Jew's" daughter!

Jessica plays off the term "bastard" and declares that if this were true, she would indeed be a "bastard" for she would then be punished for the sins of her mother as well!

Launcelet confirms she's damned by both sides – Scylla the father and Charybdis the mother – you're finished both ways.

Jessica however (now sporting an ornate cross which she displays to Launcelet) confidently asserts that she has been "saved" by her husband who has made her a Christian.

So much the worse, says Launcelet, we've had enough Christians already – even to the extent they could stand to live near each other! Making new Christians will raise the price of hogs! If we all become pork-eaters, you won't be able to get a piece of bacon on the grill at any price!

Enter LORENZO.

Jessica jibes with Launcelet threatening to tell her husband, Lorenzo, what he's said, by way of announcing his arrival.

Lorenzo, having partly taken in the scene and finding harassment of Launcelet to be an amusing pastime, warns him, tongue in cheek, that if he continues to have such intimate conversations with his wife, he just might grow jealous – and we wouldn't want that now, would we?

Jessica assuages Lorenzo telling him that he has nothing to fear about the two of them since they argue like cats and dogs and agree on nothing. Moreover, Launcelet told her she won't get into heaven because she's the Jew's daughter, and not only that, he thinks you're not a good citizen of the commonwealth – your efforts to convert Jews to Christianity only raise the price of pork!

Lorenzo, starts to get personal, telling Launcelet that he has less to account for to the nation than him, having "knocked-up" one of Portia's Moorish/African servants, which initiates a sardonic war of words between them.

Launcelet, in his inimitable way, plays with the word "Moor", suggesting that it is regrettable that there is "more" of the Moor than there should be (her being pregnant), but even if she's a less than virtuous woman she's a lot better than he first thought!

Lorenzo greets Launcelet's glib evasion with the quip that it seems every fool now knows how to deftly play with words; that soon only silence will be the mark of superior intelligence, and discourse will only be appropriate to parrots. He commands Launcelet to order the kitchen to prepare for dinner.

Launcelet replies it's already done. Everyone is hungry. Then tell them to prepare the dinner, declares Lorenzo.

That's also done, sir. I think the word you want is "cover" ("set the table"). "Will you cover then, sir?", Lorenzo responds in exasperation.

Launcelet quips jocularly that he won't because he knows his place (employing a double-entendre: "cover" meaning also to don his hat – something forbidden in the presence of his master).

Lorenzo is no match for his flippant servant, his barrage of mockery is too much to handle. In exasperation, he demands that he understand a straightforward man at his word, which he spells out explicitly: go to the servants, have them cover (set) the table, serve the meat, and we'll all come to dinner.

Undeterred, Launcelet responds with a parting shot according to his own preference. As regards the table, sir, dinner will be served on it, the meat will be served in covered dishes, as for your coming to dinner, it will be as and when you feel like it!

Exit LAUNCELET.

Watching Launcelet go, Lorenzo remarks on his remarkable ability to twist words in senseless repartee. The twit has learned a battalion of big words which he uses to defy his master, and he knows many such tricksters employed in better places that do the same. But how are you Jessica, my sweet? Tell me how you like Lord Bassanio's new wife?

Jessica replies that words don't do her justice. That Lord Bassanio must live a virtuous life blessed with a wife like Portia and have heavenly bliss here on Earth because of her. And if he is not worthy of such joy with her in the temporal world, he'll never achieve it in Heaven, either. If there were two gods that gambled and used two mortal women as their stakes – Portia being one – there would have to be something of additional value added to the other, for there is none her equal.

Lorenzo, with affection, and a bit of self-flattery, compares himself to Portia, declaring that he will be as good a husband as she is a wife. To which Jessica, perhaps playfully, perhaps staking out her independence, replies that she will determine that!

Having been thus rebuked by his prospective spouse, Lorenzo retreats, advocating that they take up the question after dinner.

Curiously, Jessica suddenly reverses her position rejecting this idea, too, desiring to show her admiration and affection while she's in the mood to do so.

Lorenzo, slightly put off by her vacillation, refuses to submit to her request, suggesting whatever she has to say should be over dinner, so that irrespective of what she says it will go down with the food.

To which, Jessica replies that she'll serve him up as if he were on the menu!

[This interchange is interesting beyond the realm of mere badinage for it may presage a source of tension in the relationship of these two idyllic lovers, as yet unarticulated, that will be seen at the end of the play. At least, it reflects a capacity for independence or perhaps a certain spitefulness on the part of Jessica consistent with the extremes to which she has gone in reaction to her father.]

Exeunt.

ACT FOUR

[4.1a – insert]

King David Hotel, Jerusalem (exterior), South Wing housing British Military administration.

Projection screens suddenly come alive with screaming headlines regarding the Shylock/Antonio trial. The stage rapidly fills with contentious crowds reflecting militant points of view pro and con as well as curious onlookers drawn by the drama unfolding outside the offices of the British military administration in Palestine. The air is thick with anticipation and tension (à la Dreyfus trial).

Amid the crowd is a young Mizrachi boy with a penetrating upper range voice and strong Mizrachi accent (characterised by the guttural "ayin" vowel heard prominently in the name Yediot) hawking Ma'ariv/Yediot newspapers. Customers appear plentiful.

Factional divides are much in evidence with left-wing demonstrators denouncing Shylock as a terrorist squaring off against Revisionists promoting anti-British agitation. Fights break out. British police move in to separate the parties, truncheons much in evidence.

Suddenly, doors to the building, heavily guarded by British military police, swing open and the crowds surge forward redirecting their attention to the task of securing seats for the proceedings.

(Cut to interior.)

We now see the hall being used by the British military tribunal packed with a diversity of interested parties, tensions running high. Antonio's comrades are seated prominently in the galleries, with Gratiano, by virtue of his thinly veiled jocularity and body language reminiscent of a "good ol' boy" at the trial of a black man in the South, particularly conspicuous.

Among the crowd we see once again the Germans in the company of their Arab "friends", members of the press, foreign visitors, a variety of social types — workers, businessmen, ladies of fashion, labour and revisionist political cadres, intellectuals — all intensely focused on the proceedings at hand.

And once more we see the young "Irgunists" enter the room, taking up positions anonymously among the crowd, carefully avoiding recognition as a group...

4.1 – Shylock's Rage

King David Hotel, Jerusalem (interior), South Wing housing British Military Tribunal.

Enter the GENERAL (DUKE), Military Officers, ANTONIO, BASSANIO, GRATIANO, SALARIO, and others.

Shakespeare's Duke, for our purposes, will either be a distinguished looking, greying British General and Governor of Palestine whose benevolent exterior cloaks a grudging intolerance and distaste for the Jews, or a sharp-featured weasel of a man of malevolent charm reminiscent of Olivier's Richard III, which a real Governor, and reputed antisemite, Lieutenant General Sir Louis Jean Bols, resembled (see note 1 on page 211). It is apparent upon his entry to the court that he is hardened in his antipathy towards Shylock and the proceedings themselves, but powerless under the law to stop them.

He and his entourage of judges and eminent figures of Palestine/Venice take their seats. He calls for Antonio, who acknowledges his presence. The General then proceeds to express his thoroughgoing sympathy for Antonio's predicament facing, as he does, in the opinion of the court, an implacable enemy devoid of humanity, pity, or mercy.

Antonio, fully embracing the role of martyr, thanks the General for his strenuous efforts to dissuade Shylock, out-of-court, to abandon his suit. But since Shylock remains adamant and the law offers no immediate avenue to escape his charges, he will oppose his rage and extremism with quiet forbearance.

The General then orders that "the Jew" be brought into court.

Salario declares that he is waiting outside the door and here he comes.

Enter SHYLOCK.

Shylock slowly enters the court with a haughty air and crazed look about him.

The General orders that room be made for Shylock to stand before him. He then addresses him with thinly veiled contempt and an air of intimidation in the guise of a humanitarian appeal:

Popular opinion sides with his own: Shylock is only pursuing this cruel charade for dramatic effect, and that at the last moment (if he knows what's good for him) he'll relent and show a mercy even stranger than his prior cruelty. That despite being here to collect the penalty – a pound of flesh – he'll not only forgo the penalty, but in a spirit of love and humanity sacrifice some portion of the principle owed as well, turning a compassionate eye on the oppressive losses that have recently befallen the merchant. Losses substantial enough to drive even the most distinguished trader to bankruptcy and make even the most insensitive and cruel Tartar or Turk – unused to shows of sympathy – express compassion for him. Moreover—the General admonishes Shylock bluntly—all are expecting cooperation and sympathy, *Jew*...

Not to be denied or deterred from his course, Shylock replies that he's fully disclosed his intentions to the General, and, moreover, has taken an oath by his Holy Sabbath to "have the due and forfeit of (his) bond". And if the court fails to uphold these legally binding claims it will undermine the constitution of the city and its freedoms.

Anticipating the court's objections, Shylock asserts, you may ask why I'd rather have a measure of rotten flesh than three thousand ducats? I'll not answer that except to say that it pleases me. Is that answer enough? What if my house was infested with a rat and I decided to pay ten thousand ducats to have it eradicated – does that answer your question?

He further expounds: some men detest roast pig. Some are enraged when they see a cat. And some wet themselves when they hear bagpipes play! It's irrational, a matter of passion, which determines what one likes or hates. So, in answer to your question, since there is no good reason why he can't tolerate a roast pig; why he can't stand an inoffensive cat; why he is humiliated by fouling himself at the sound of woollen bagpipes – so I cannot justify, nor will not justify – more than a deep-seated hatred and loathing for Antonio that impels this worthless suit against him. Are you satisfied now?

That's no answer, cries Bassanio, to justify your cruelty and heartlessness! "I am not obliged to please thee with my answers", Shylock retorts!

"Do all men kill the things they do not love?" Bassanio enquires. "Hates any man the thing he would not kill?" Shylock parries. Not all displeasure starts out as hate, counters Bassanio. What? Should you let a snake sting twice?!! Comes Shylock's response.

Antonio, in a state of resignation, begs Bassanio not to argue further with "the Jew". It is as futile as standing on the beach and asking the tide to abate or questioning the wolf why he made the ewe grieve by killing her lamb. You might as well restrain the pines on the mountain top from rustling in the wind or do anything more futile than try to moderate – what could be harder? – his Jewish heart. Therefore, I beg you, make no further proposals or pursue other alternatives, but let me have swift judgment and "the Jew" his wish.

In a last-ditch effort Bassanio offers Shylock six thousand ducats rather than three. To which Shylock responds emphatically, that if the six thousand ducats were multiplied by six, he would not take them. He would have his penalty.

The General intervenes demanding of Shylock how he could expect mercy if he offers none.

Shylock's response is sharp and legally correct; what judgment does he have to fear if he's done nothing wrong? But his defence now takes on a larger critique of the corruption of the state and the society that has oppressed him. He confronts the court with society's history of slavery in which many present own slaves whom they use like asses, dogs, and mules, performing degrading work just because they bought them. What if I tell you, Shylock declares, "Let them be free! Marry them to your heirs! Why sweat they under burdens? Let their beds be made as soft as yours and let their palates be seasoned with such viands?" You will respond that the slaves are yours!! And I will respond likewise. The pound of flesh that I claim from him was purchased at a high price, it is mine and I will have it! If you deny my claim, a curse upon your laws, the laws of Venice/Palestine have no authority. I demand justice. Tell me, will I get it?

The General, clearly unwilling to engage the legal challenge posed by Shylock, declares his authority to dismiss the court unless a learned Doctor of Laws, Bellario, arrives that day to judge the matter.

Salario calls to the bench that a messenger has arrived with letters from the doctor, Bellario, who has just arrived from Padua.

The General calls for the letters and the messenger.

Bassanio seeks to buoy Antonio, encouraging him to buck up and have courage, declaring the Jew will have his own "flesh, blood, bones, and all" before Antonio will lose one drop of blood on his account.

In a state of morose self-pity, Antonio declares himself the sick sheep of the flock who most deserves to die. The weakest fruit falls first to the ground, says he – allow me to do the same. The best prospect for you, Bassanio, is to continue living and devote yourself to writing my epitaph for posterity.

Enter NERISSA, disguised as a clerk.

The General inquires if she has come from Padua and Bellario.

Yes, she replies, and extends Bellario's greetings *(giving the General a letter).*

(SHYLOCK sharpens a knife on the bottom of his shoe.)

Bassanio confronts Shylock by asking why he is sharpening his knife so intently. Shylock states his intent to cut his loss from that bankrupt merchant there.

Gratiano interjects from the gallery that Shylock, heartless Jew, sharpens his knife not on the sole of his shoe but upon his soul in Heaven. No metal – not even the hangman's axe – can yield half the sharpness of his malice. Can no prayers touch you?

No, snaps Shylock – his desire for confrontation with the crudest of his nemeses in full bloom – none that you have intelligence enough to make, you ignoramus!

Infuriated by the Jews temerity, Gratiano holds forth with a stream of invective – unmoderated by the bench – damning Shylock and calling him a repulsive dog who deserves to be slaughtered. Gratiano declares that Shylock almost makes him doubt his faith as a Christian (whatever that means in view of his manifold chauvinisms and bigotries) and embrace the view of Pythagoras that the souls of animals can invade the bodies of men. That the vicious cur-soul of a wolf, hanged for human carnage, escaped to the womb of Shylock's unholy mother, and implanted itself in him before birth; for his behaviours "are wolvish, bloody, starved, and ravenous".

Shylock parries Gratiano's hyperbole, admonishing him that until he can rant away Antonio's signature, he's just abusing his lungs by raving so vehemently. Imperiously, Shylock advises "good-boy" Gratiano to hold his tongue lest his mind be reduced to ruin beyond repair. Shylock declares he stands with the law on his side.

The General, who had been perusing the documents which arrived from Padua while this set-to proceeded, now interrupts the proceedings asking if "a young and learned doctor" recommended in the letter is present in the court. "Where is he?"

Nerissa answers that he is nearby awaiting admission to the court.

The General responds that he's welcome "with all (his) heart", and requests three or four representatives of the court go to welcome him. In the meantime, the court shall hear Bellario's letter: *(reads)*

(The letter relates that Bellario is presently very ill, but upon learning of the case regarding Antonio and Shylock has – together with a young lawyer from Rome, Balthasar, who was attending him – examined the case and performed extensive research. That young lawyer is fully acquainted with Bellario's opinion of the case and augmented by his own learned opinion – which he cannot praise too highly – has come to fulfil your lordship's request on Bellario's behalf. Bellario begs you not to allow his youth to disqualify his judgment, "for [he] never knew so young a body with so old a head". He hopes you will accept him warmly and that the trial will better demonstrate his exceptional qualities).

Enter PORTIA disguised as BALTHASAR, a Judge.

You've heard what the learned Bellario has written. And here I believe is the learned Doctor, himself. "Give me your hand. Come you from old Bellario?"

Balthasar confirms that he did.

The General confirms his welcome and invites Balthasar to "take [his] place". He inquires if he is acquainted with the points of contention that bring the case before the court.

Balthasar affirms that he is fully familiar with the case, and in an effort to further validate his status as an outside observer asks that the plaintiff and the defendant be identified – "Which is the merchant here, and which the Jew?" (As if 'he' doesn't know already).

The General calls Antonio and old Shylock forth before the bench. Balthasar enquires of Shylock if Shylock is, indeed, his name.

Shylock replies that it is his name.

Balthasar observes that his suit is of a strange character. But one which the Venetian law cannot challenge as you pursue it.

(He turns to Antonio) He has a case against you, does he not? Yes, Antonio admits, so he says.

Do you admit the validity of the contract? asks Balthasar. Antonio admits that he does.

"Then must the Jew be merciful", declares Balthasar.

"On what compulsion must I? Tell me that," replies Shylock.

Portia, born of a class largely concerned with mercy only for themselves, proceeds in her guise as Balthasar to lecture Shylock on mercy's fine points thus: It is not forced. It drops like gentle rain upon the ground beneath. And it is doubly blessed: blessing the giver as well as the taker. Mercy is strongest in the powerful. It complements the image of a king more than his crown. The king's sceptre shows the force of his earthly power inspiring wonderment and authority, in which resides the fear of kings. But mercy is higher still and more powerful than the force of the sceptre. Its throne resides in the hearts of kings, a quality of God himself. And earthly power most resembles godliness when "mercy seasons justice". Therefore, Jew, though you are demanding justice, consider that justice alone will not achieve for us salvation. We pray for mercy, and that same prayer teaches us to practice acts of mercy. I have spoken this way in hope of moderating the justice of your cause which this strict court will be obliged to enforce against the merchant there.

In response, Shylock declares full responsibility for his actions which demand "the law, the penalty, and forfeit of my bond".

Balthasar enquires if Antonio is unable to pay back the debt.

Bassanio, in a frenzy, intervenes by offering to pay the bond immediately in court – in fact twice the sum, and if that is not enough, he'll commit to pay it ten times over with his hands, head, and heart as collateral. If this is still insufficient, then it shows that evil conquers all.

Bassanio begs the General to use his power, just this once, to moderate the law. "To do a great right, do a little wrong, and curb this cruel devil of his will."

But Balthasar will have none of it arguing that no power in Venice/Palestine can change an established order. It will establish a precedent that will result in many poor legal judgments affecting the state. It must not be.

Shylock is elated, comparing Balthasar to a young Daniel of the Bible, noted for his wisdom, "come to judgment", effusively declaring how he honours him. Balthasar asks to see the contract. *(Giving Balthasar a document)* Shylock, now convinced that Balthasar is inclined in his favour, eagerly offers him the document.

Balthasar, perusing the contract, remarks to Shylock that he's now being offered three times the amount he's owed.

But this only triggers in Shylock a return to the mania he exhibited in the streets obsessively declaring he has an oath made in Heaven to follow through with his demand for Antonio's flesh which he dares not violate – to do so would lay perjury upon his soul which he will not do even for Venice/Palestine.

Balthasar, knowingly, with a trick up "his" sleeve, dramatically declares that the contract is in default. And as a result, "the Jew may claim a pound of flesh to be by him cut off nearest the merchant's heart" – but be merciful, he implores him, take three times your money and have me tear up the contract.

But appeals to Shylock only fuel his obduracy coming as they do from those who have so long been devoid of compassion for him. Knowing he has the law on his side at Antonio's expense eliminates all restraints upon him and opens the floodgates of pent-up humiliations, resentments, and dysfunctions long repressed.

Shylock responds, with growing and observable agitation, that the contract will be torn up when the debt is paid in accordance with its terms. Still of the impression he has the upper hand with Balthasar, Shylock compliments him as "a worthy judge" who knows the law. He terms his presentation "most sound" and as a distinguished pillar of the law he bids him to render his judgment, for "by my soul I swear there is no power in the tongue of man to alter me. I stay here on my bond".

Antonio concurs in exhaustion and resignation that judgment be rendered. Balthasar responds that the verdict requires the merchant to prepare his chest for the knife. Shylock ecstatically lauds the "noble judge" and "excellent young man!".

Balthasar continues his judgment that the law justifies the penalty which now appears due under the terms of the contract.

Shylock's enthusiasm knows no bounds. He praises Balthasar's wisdom and righteousness and complements him on his maturity which far exceeds his youthful appearance (but even in his praise a growing element of mania and instability equal to his periods of condemnation become apparent).

Balthasar orders Antonio to bare his chest.

Shylock is now slipping into a state of frenzy with the approach of his murderous goal. He maniacally confirms the Judge's order. Yes, the contract says the chest, nearest to the heart – yes, that's what it says, does it not "noble judge"? The exact words.
Balthasar, with great formality, asks if there is a scale present to weigh the flesh. Shylock confirms he has one ready.

Balthasar then orders Shylock to provide a surgeon ready to close Antonio's wounds to prevent him bleeding to death.

Shylock is taken aback and questions whether that obligation is required by the contract.

Balthasar states that it is not written there but that it would be good for him to do it for charity's sake.

Shylock intently examining the document declares that he can't find such a requirement contained there.

Balthasar ignores him and addresses Antonio, asking if he has anything to say.

Antonio says he has little to say, that he is prepared for death, and asks Bassanio for his hand as he bids him farewell.

[Note: If there is any doubt about the justification for the current fashion of assuming a gay relationship between Antonio and Bassanio the following speech should put it to rest.]

With sorrow and what can be seen here as resentment for Bassanio's liaison with Portia, Antonio manipulatively gets in his final "dig" by "selflessly" telling his "friend" not to grieve about the fact that he has fallen to this fate because of [him]! He further rationalises that "Fortune" has been kinder to him than most by sparing him the prospect of outliving his wealth and living on in withered old age and poverty – a fate from which he will now be freed. He requests Bassanio send his greetings to his "honourable wife", Portia, and relate to her how he met his end. Tell her how deeply I loved you. Speak well of me after I'm gone. And when all is said, have her judge "Whether Bassanio had not once a love". Regret only that you will lose your "friend" – he doesn't regret that he's paid your debt (reminding him again!). "For if the Jew do cut but deep enough, I'll pay it presently with all my heart."

Bassanio extravagantly reciprocates his devotion to Antonio, declaring that his wife is as dear to him as life itself, but life itself, his wife, and the entire world are not dearer to him than Antonio's life. "I would lose all—ay, sacrifice them all here to this devil—to deliver you."

(Portia, through the character of Balthasar, on suddenly seeing a side of her "beloved" she wasn't quite aware of, makes the aside, disapprovingly, that his wife might not be altogether appreciative of his sentiments if she were there to hear them!)

At which point Gratiano, crudely as usual, and ever eager to walk in Bassanio's shoes, puts in his two cents, insisting that he has a wife whom he loves but who he'd rather see in heaven so she could engage some higher power to change the mind of this "Jew-dog".

Nerissa, disguised as Balthasar's clerk, caustically remarks to Portia under her breath, that it's well he's offering her as a sacrifice behind her back or that wish could seriously upset their domestic tranquility.

Shylock, observing these duplicities, declares in a sudden moment of clarity and sobriety that this is typical of Christian husbands – that he has a daughter who he would prefer married any descendent of the thief Barabbas than a Christian! But just as suddenly his focus and obsessions return, and he demands of the Judge that they waste no further time and proceed to sentencing.

Balthasar confirms the sentence; a pound of the merchant's flesh is his, the court grants it, and the law approves it.

In near ecstasy Shylock proclaims the Judge's virtue and prepares to move on Antonio.

[Insert]

With a disapproving grimace and nod the General engages three beefy RMPs (Royal Military Police) who go about with unemotional precision restraining Antonio in a heavy chair brought to the centre of the court for purposes of administering his sentence. An Anglican bishop briefly accompanies him administering perfunctory last rights and quickly withdrawing. The MPs then unceremoniously rip open his shirt revealing his left breast – dramatically demonstrating that under the laws of Venice/Palestine indignity can be had by all under military constraint. The courtroom is transfixed in a state of perverse anticipation of imminent bloodshed. As the proceedings unfold, we see a dark-haired young woman, identity veiled by a dark headscarf, quietly enter the back of the courtroom her presence hidden by a pillar. Nervously, she fingers a cross about her neck as she intently takes in the proceedings.

Now that the moment of truth has arrived Shylock's mind descends into an emotional maelstrom. Up to now, it has been one thing to rant and wish the mutilation and death of Antonio as an abstraction, a fantasy, but now that Shylock has the power within his hands to actually effect it, he enters into a state of crisis and indecision he never anticipated.

In all his life Shylock has never killed so much as a fly, now he is on the verge of committing a murderous assault that contradicts every value that defines him as a Jew, for whom mutilation and murder are anathema. Murderous revenge, in his mind, has always been the province of the "Goyim" – a perversity he has envied in his worst moments, but never dreamt he could practice. At some level of his being he knows that despite its dreadful appeal it is a poisoned chalice from which he dares not drink. Yet, the force of circumstance now drives him on to this abhorrent goal.

Brandishing his well-sharpened blade, Shylock, in a state of trepidation, draws near to Antonio. Trembling, he summons up the strength to follow through with his murderous design. The moment is suspended in a state of tension that electrifies and transfixes the court room and is reflected in the sudden onset of paralysis on the part of Shylock revealing a state of raging internal conflict palpable in its pain and intensity.

Despite his misgivings, Shylock, slowly, inexorably approaches Antonio, knife in hand, positioned for amputation of the promised "pound of flesh". But his internal struggle reaches the breaking point as he nears his target. He falters, swoons, stumbles back in nervous indecision.

Then, suddenly, in a final moment of fury and resolve, he shifts the weapon to a stabbing position with both hands above his head as he rapidly advances upon Antonio. But on the verge of striking the death blow, Shylock falters once again. Lacking the will to take Antonio's life, and retreating from his threat that, "the villainy you teach me, I will execute", he doesn't have it in him to administer the coup de grâce, no matter his complaint.

The burden of his anguish and pain overwhelms him to breaking point. He can bear it no longer. Life on so many levels offers him no resolve, not even the revenge he so ardently sought *and now has so close at hand. The knife, as if channelling his subliminal thoughts, shifts suddenly in his hands as he stands a sobbing "angel of death". Emitting the agonising howl of a wounded beast, the blade shifts in his own direction hovering in deadly menace above both men in excruciating indecision as to which target it will strike – Antonio for revenge or himself for deliverance.*

Then the hand of Balthasar forcefully interdicts the fatal blow.

(The packed courtroom breathes relief. And the mystery woman in black hides her face in stifled sobs by her pillar, nervously clutching the cross about her neck.)

"Tarry a little," Balthasar admonishes Shylock. There's another thing. This contract doesn't give you one drop of blood. The terms are specifically, "a pound of flesh". Thus, you may take your bond, your pound of flesh, but if you shed one drop of Christian blood in the process, your lands and possessions will be legally seized by the state.

Gratiano, with mocking delight, mimics Shylock's praise for Balthasar, "O upright judge! – Mark, Jew. – O learnèd judge!"

Stunned, Shylock stumbles back weakly querying if that is the law?

Balthasar tells him he can read the act for himself, and since he demanded "justice" he can now be certain he'll get more of it than he bargained for.

Gratiano continues his mockery "O upright judge, etc."

Stunned by his sudden reversal of fortune, Shylock, now realising his vulnerability, in confusion and panic retreats from his designs on Antonio and offers to accept the previous offer – he'll take three times the amount of the loan and let the Christian go.

Bassanio quickly offers him the money while the opportunity is ripe.

But Balthasar demands restraint – no need to rush – declaring gravely that "the Jew" desires "justice" and he shall have it, only the "penalty" nothing more.

Gratiano's delight and mockery knows no bounds, "O learnèd judge! – Mark, Jew, a learnèd judge!".

Balthasar demands that Shylock prepare to return to the grisly business he has retreated from with the proviso that he "shed no blood" in the process nor cut more nor less than a pound exactly. If he fails to precisely take a pound of flesh, even by the smallest increment, he will die, and all his property will be confiscated by the state.

Gratiano continues his mockery: "A second Daniel! – A Daniel, Jew! Now, infidel, I have you on the hip."

Balthasar, now with a demeanour rather removed from Portia's lately extolled "quality of mercy", confronts Shylock demanding to know why he hesitates, why he doesn't take his penalty?

Shylock, whimpering, pleads for his money and release from the proceedings.

Eager to end the agony for Antonio, Bassanio, ready with the money, once again offers to pay Shylock immediately.

Once again, Balthasar denies it, declaring that Shylock has already refused payment before the court and now he will only have "justice and his bond".

"A Daniel, still say I, a second Daniel! – I thank thee, Jew, for teaching me that word", Gratiano's mockery continues.

Shylock, now devoid of leverage, implores Balthasar for, at least, the return of his principle, which the latter, with steely disdain, denies him. He will have nothing, but the penalty taken at his peril.

Shylock declares the Devil take him, he'll stay and argue no longer!

But the disguised Portia is not through with him yet, nor is her "quality of mercy" raining in his direction. Balthasar demands that he wait, for he claims he has run afoul of another statute which has a hold on him. According to the law, if it is proven that an "alien" tries directly or indirectly to take the life of a citizen, the victim may take one half of his property, the other half goes to the state and the life of the offender lies in the hands of the General, without appeal. He maintains that Shylock is in violation of the statute for it clearly appears through the current proceedings that both indirectly and directly Shylock has contrived to take the life of the defendant, Antonio, and has earned the punishment he has described. He orders him, therefore, to kneel before the General and beg him for mercy (rather than waiting for it to "drop as the gentle rain from heaven upon the place beneath").

With his vindictiveness and bigotry on full display, Gratiano continues his calumnies, telling Shylock to beg leave to hang himself! But then again if his property is confiscated by the state he won't have the price of a rope, so he'll be hanged at government expense!

The General, observably weary of the convoluted case before him, imperiously declares that in the spirit of a superior Christian ethic he will pardon Shylock even before he appeals for it; that half his holdings will be Antonio's and the remainder will go to the state – the sum of which may be reduced to a fine if Shylock demonstrates appropriate humility.

Balthasar interjects that such a reduction would apply only to the state not to the penalty forthcoming to Antonio.

Shylock, in a state of resentment and despair, tells the court not to pardon his life. They take his house when they take the means by which he supports his house; they take his life when they take the source of his livelihood.

Balthasar enquires of Antonio what "mercy" he would be willing to show Shylock. A free hangman's rope, Gratiano interjects.

Antonio "magnanimously" replies that he is content if the state sets aside half of Shylock's property, provided he is given the other half in trust to bequeath upon his death to the man who "recently stole his daughter". And to cap it off, Antonio adds two more provisos: first, that for this courtesy Shylock must immediately become a Christian; second, that he makes out a will before the court leaving all in his possessions to his son-in-law Lorenzo and his daughter.

The General confirms these obligations threatening to retract the pardon just pronounced if they are not met. Balthasar, with thinly veiled satisfaction, asks Shylock if he is satisfied, and what he has to say?

Devastated, Shylock, in utter dejection, whispers his consent.

Balthasar orders his clerk (Nerissa), to draw up a deed confirming his gift.

In a state of shock and near collapse, Shylock pathetically begs leave of the court, requesting that they send the document to him which he will sign.

The General, glad to be finally rid of this unpleasant affair, releases him further admonishing Shylock to be sure to follow through on his commitment to sign.

Gratiano's bigotry and vindictiveness continue unabated, his parting shot to Shylock that if it were up to him as judge, rather than two godfathers at his christening he'd give him ten more for a jury to send him to a hanging rather than "the font".

Exit SHYLOCK.

The tension of the courtroom is broken in various ways by various factions. Antonio and Bassanio embrace and are joined in congratulations by the others of their group. Portia stands slightly dazed by the success of her charade as Balthasar and her desire to reconnect with Bassanio (not least to give him a piece of her mind regarding his personal "priorities") which must still be stifled.

The mystery woman by the pillar tries to contain herself. Her scarf momentarily drops before fleeing the hall. It is Jessica...

The General, most impressed by Balthasar's legal prowess, and most appreciative of his service to the court relieving him of an onerous task beyond his expertise, cordially invites him to dinner.

Eager to exit the scene, Balthasar begs his forgiveness with the excuse that he must travel to Padua that evening and must leave.

The General expresses his regret that he hasn't time to join him. In parting he orders Antonio to give Balthasar a reward for his services for which he is much beholden to him.

Exit GENERAL and his train.

Bassanio, with great appreciation for Balthasar's legal expertise which has saved his friend from some terrible punishments (and still in the dark regarding the masquerade going on before him) offers him the three thousand ducats that was owed to Shylock in thanks for his generous efforts.

And Antonio pledges above and beyond financial reward their debt and "love and service evermore."

Balthasar magnanimously declines their offer declaring that a goal well-achieved is satisfaction enough, and saving Antonio is sufficient – he never was concerned about the money. With a bit of devilish humour, lost on Bassanio, he also expresses the hope he will recognise him when they meet again, wishing him well and goodbye.

Bassanio, increasingly attracted to this mysterious Balthasar, will hear none of it, and insists that he take some gift from them as a token of thanks rather than a payment. He begs Balthasar to grant him two wishes: first, not to refuse him, and second, to pardon his insistence.

Portia senses the possibility to test her new husband's fidelity and honesty while having a bit of mischievous fun at his expense. Balthasar acquiesces to his demand to accept a token of their gratitude, requesting Antonio's gloves, which he will wear in his honour. And in a remembrance of his affection, he requests Bassanio's ring. Bassanio reflexively withdraws his hand, but is admonished by Balthasar not to do so, that he will take no more than the ring which he cannot now deny him.

Bassanio tries to finesse his way out of the predicament, claiming that the ring is but a mere trinket not worthy of the Judge's status and achievements – he will not embarrass himself by giving him such inadequate recompense.

Bassanio's ploy fails miserably, with Balthasar digging in his heels demanding that he wants only the ring now and is adamant in that desire.

Bassanio candidly asserts that the ring itself is more important than its monetary value. He promises to find for Balthasar the most expensive ring in Venice/Palestine by means of a public announcement but begs his forgiveness to forego the ring in question.

Balthasar remains unmollified, confronting him aggressively with the rejoinder that he likes to make offers freely. First, he taught how to beg and now is teaching how a beggar should be answered!

Bassanio protests that the ring was given to him by his wife who made him swear that he would neither sell, give away, nor lose it.

Balthasar resentfully dismisses his argument as just another excuse men use to avoid gift-giving. If his wife is not totally deranged, she will appreciate how much he deserves the ring and would not be angry forever with him giving it to him. Wishing him peace (and a measure of guilt) he and his clerk, Nerissa, abruptly take their leave.

Exeunt PORTIA/BALTHASAR and NERISSA/CLERK.

Upon their exit, Antonio prevails upon Bassanio to give Balthasar the ring – weighing the lawyer's achievements and his own affection against Portia's orders.

(Gives GRATIANO the ring.)

Bassanio reluctantly gives Gratiano the ring ordering him to quickly run after the departing attorney, present him with the ring as a gift, and bring him, if possible, to Antonio's house.

Exit GRATIANO.

Embracing Antonio, Bassanio affectionately suggests they presently repair to his home, and early the next morning dash to Belmont.

Exeunt.

4.2

A street in Jerusalem by the courthouse.

Enter PORTIA and NERISSA, both disguised.

As they approach a waiting limousine, Portia instructs Nerissa to find the Jew's house and give him the deed for the court and have him sign it. She tells her they will leave that evening and be home a day before their husbands return. And what a pleasant surprise this deed will be for Lorenzo.

Enter GRATIANO (giving PORTIA BASSANIO'S ring).

Gratiano manages to overtake the two as they enter the car. Glad that he managed to catch them, he tells Balthasar that upon further reflection Bassanio wishes him to have the ring after all as well as an invitation to dinner.

Balthasar begs off the dinner invitation without further elaboration, but thankfully accepts the ring. He requests Gratiano convey his thanks to Bassanio and show his clerk the way to Shylock's house.

Gratiano agrees to do so.

Nerissa, returned to her role as clerk, officiously requests to speak to her master privately. In an aside to Portia, she expresses her intention to duplicate Portia's mischief with her own husband,

Gratiano, and see if she can also get the ring that he promised not to part with.

Portia, amused at her plan, expresses confidence she'll succeed and that the two dupes will swear they gave the rings to men – but the two of them will face them down and swear more convincingly to the contrary!! – But quickly go now, she tells her, you know where I'll be waiting for you.

Nerissa then asks Gratiano to show her the way to Shylock's house.

Exeunt.

[Note: Jessica enters Act 5 a shaken and ambivalent woman caught between her past rebellion and hope for liberation from her father, and her growing doubts about her status among the gentiles. The devastation of her father, and the profound indignity of the forced conversion imposed upon him by the "genteel folk" with whom she now resides, has cast a pall over her apostasy, which, in Act 5 starts to colour her relationship with Lorenzo.]

ACT FIVE

5.1

A beach on the coast of Palestine.

The scene opens with two contrasting elements: the voice of Lorenzo in darkness uttering the opening of his speech, "The moon shines bright. In such a night as this, when the sweet wind did gently kiss the trees and they did make no noise...", while visually, under the light of that brilliant moon we see the projected image of an Aliyah Bet illegal immigrant ship off the coast of Palestine with a long, thick mooring rope extending to shore supporting the landing of desperate water-soaked refugees aided by scantily clad Haganah underground forces.

Once established, the scene freezes in tableau as focus shifts to a veranda where we find Lorenzo and Jessica alone together in amorous embrace (Lorenzo enfolds her from behind, while Jessica, receptive to a point, exhibits a certain hesitant resistance – an ambivalence that advances during the scene).

The juxtaposition of these images punctuates the dichotomy between the idyllic condition of the British ruling class there and the brutal realities of Jewish refugee rescue unfolding on Palestine's shores under the same brilliant moon.

Lorenzo affectionately waxes poetic but does so with a strangely equivocal subtext citing the figure of Troilus betrayed by his lover,

Cressida, foreshadowing a certain ambivalence beginning to creep into the Jessica/Lorenzo relationship.

Jessica's reaction to this affront citing a doomed classical romance, further deepens the divide. By alluding to the myth of Thisbe and Pyramus, in which Thisbe escapes an approaching lion only to have Pyramus mistakenly take his own life thinking her killed by the beast, she provocatively questions the integrity of Lorenzo's own love for her.

In response, Lorenzo references Dido holding a willow branch by the sea begging her lover, Aeneas return to Carthage – an image, yet again, of love unrequited.

And Jessica, not to be outdone, cites Medea, gathering enchanted herbs to aid her lover Jason's father, Aeson, prior to his betrayal of her and her subsequent murder of their children in revenge – upping the emotional ante.

To which Lorenzo, amid ostensibly amorous banter, with more than a passive-aggressive twist, replies that "in such a night" Jessica stole from the rich Jew, Shylock, and ran away with her profligate lover all the way to Belmont! A remarkably insensitive reference clouding their interchange by "rubbing in" Jessica's "alien" origins and the memory of her father's unhappy fate – emphasising once again, that even in their private moments she must remember that Christianity is triumphant, and not forget her inferior status as a "trophy-wife" of the dominant culture (for which Jessica may be having second thoughts).

With thinly veiled ambivalence Jessica responds that "in such a night" Lorenzo won her heart with many professions of devotion, none of which was true! ... (What are we to make of that?)

Lorenzo, clearly oblivious to the gravity of his provocations which initiated the exchange, fatuously protests that "in such a night" lovely Jessica, like an ill-tempered fury, wrongly accused her lover – but he, in good "Christian" fashion, extended his "forgiveness" for her "injustice" to him. *Plus ça change, plus c'est la même chose!*

Through this equivocal literary game, a provocative subtext of emotional uncertainty suddenly emerges clouding the true nature of their romance and suggesting darker implications for their future together.

Jessica, hearing approaching footsteps, cuts off the competition admonishing Lorenzo that she would "outnight" him yet, were it not that someone was coming – at which she breaks away to a discreet distance from him.

Enter STEPHANO, a messenger.

Stephano announces the imminent return of Portia to Belmont in the early hours of the morning. He relates that she presently remains at the monastery in devotion and supplication for a blessed marriage.

Lorenzo enquires who is accompanying her. To which Stephano replies that she is in the company of a "holy hermit and her maid" and inquires if Bassanio has yet returned.

Lorenzo replies that he hasn't and that they've heard nothing from him. He calls Jessica to accompany him to the house and prepare an elegant welcome for Portia's return.

Enter LAUNCELET.

Suddenly, unruly shouts are heard seeking Master Lorenzo. It is Launcelet Gobbo who, in his inimitable fashion, doesn't acknowledge Lorenzo even when he responds to his call and then tells him to tell Lorenzo that a messenger has arrived announcing good news and the return of Bassanio by morning! At which point he departs as abruptly and unceremoniously as he appeared!

Exit LAUNCELET.

Lorenzo appeals once again to Jessica to return to the house to await Portia's arrival. She is resistant. Sensing something is amiss, he relents saying it "doesn't matter" and questions his own suggestion – "Why should we go in?" – ordering Stephano to go in their stead, announce that Portia will soon be there, and bring musicians out into the open air.

Exit STEPHANO.

In an effort to reengage with Jessica, Lorenzo returns to a romantic and poetic tone, musing on the beauty of the bright moonlight on the slopes surrounding the veranda. He invites her to sit with him and allow the strains of sweet music to enter their ears – the quiet of the night the perfect time for its harmonies to be felt. He beckons her again to sit by him. Her resistance fading, she does so. Lorenzo continues with a magisterial description of the stars which decorate the "floor of heaven" in bright gold; even the smallest of them sings like an angel in a choir for the "young-eyed cherubim". "Immortal souls" also possess such harmonies, but encased as we are in bodies of clay, we are sadly unable to hear them.

Enter musicians.

A solo saxophone sensuously glides into a rendition of *Les Feuilles Mortes/The Autumn Leaves* picked up by other instruments and a vocalist in a jazz ensemble. A stream of guests from the house, somewhat dishevelled from a late night of partying, renew their enthusiasm at the sound of this new and very popular hit, launching into a languid display of dancing.

Lorenzo greets and encourages them to wake the moon goddess, Diana, with their melodies and bring her to them. The entertainment continues in the background as Jessica and Lorenzo continue their exchange.

Music plays.

Jessica reflects that she is never cheerful when she hears lovely music (and, perhaps, there is reason not to be now).

Lorenzo deflects her misgivings through flattery telling her that the reason for her lack of mirth is that she is so focused on and sensitive to the music itself. Just consider a wild herd of animals or a group of unbroken colts bounding and loudly neighing – which is their nature. If by chance they should hear a trumpet sound or any strain of music reach their ears, you will see them stand as one transfixed, their fierce eyes transformed and softened by the tender force of music.

That's why it was said of Ovid, the great musician, that he could bring to him "trees, stones, and floods" by his music, since there was nothing so insensitive, brutal, or furious whose character music couldn't change.

The man who has no music in him and is not inspired by beauteous harmonies is only suited for disloyalty, brutality, and plunder. His senses are numb and his passions dark as Hades. No such person can be trusted. Attend to the music. (Lorenzo encourages the musicians to strike an upbeat number, "Begin the Beguine", drawing guests enthusiastically from the house to the unfolding party and dancing on the veranda).

Enter PORTIA and NERISSA, a narrow spot of light separating them spatially from the house as they take in from a distance the goings on, the music sounding distantly in their space.

Portia observes that the light they see in the distance is burning in her hall. What a distance such a little taper can project its light! Much like kind acts in a wicked world.

Nerissa observes that when the moon was shining, they didn't notice the candle.

Portia responds that a lesser ruler appears as imposing as a king until a king is near, then his stature drains as when a small brook empties into a larger flood. "But listen! Music!" Portia declares, suddenly aware of the strains as if for the first time.

Nerissa observes that the music coming from the house is for her!

Portia is taken by how much better the melodies seem by night than by day.

Nerissa suggests that the night's silence enhances it.

Portia notes that the quality of so much in life is determined by setting. The crow sings as beautifully as the lark when no one is listening, and if the nightingale should sing by day in the company of cackling geese its song would be heard no better than the wren. "How many things by season seasoned are to their right praise and true perfection!" And the moon seems to sleep in the embrace of Endymion impervious to the disturbances of the world.

Music ceases.

Lorenzo, catching sight of Portia, abruptly signals the music to stop to the momentary confusion of the crowd, and then in a grand manner announces her arrival to the cheers of all assembled followed by the band launching into a rendition of Handel's *See the Conquering Hero Come!* sung robustly by all the guests.

Amused and slightly embarrassed by the grand reception, Portia self-deprecatingly responds, much to the delight of the house, that Lorenzo was aware of her presence "as the blind man knows the cuckoo—by the bad voice!"

Lorenzo, to the cheers of all, effusively welcomes her home.

Portia, still somewhat dazed by the emotional experience of the Shylock trial and her religious devotions in anticipation of her marriage, not yet fully realised, informs her friends she has been praying for her husband's well-being who, she hopes, has been aided by her supplications, and asks if Bassanio and Co. have returned.

Lorenzo responds that they have not, but that a messenger arrived telling them they were en route.

Portia takes aside Nerissa in the presence of Lorenzo and Jessica, orders her to tell the servants not to mention her absence and instructs Lorenzo and Jessica to do the same.

A tucket sounds.

Lorenzo announces to Portia that Bassanio draws near, and with a wink and a nod reassures her to fear not, they won't snitch on her.

Portia observes to herself, with a hint of foreboding, that the coming dawn makes the night seem like sickened daylight – only a little more pallid, like a day when the sun is hidden by clouds (what does this portend?).

Enter BASSANIO, ANTONIO, GRATIANO, and their followers.

Bassanio enters the scene with great anticipation transfixed by the sight of his new wife. The saxophone launches into a reprise of *Les Feuilles Mortes* as he grandly approaches Portia awakened from her reverie, declaring lovingly that she would bring light to the darkness were she to walk forth at night.

Portia glides towards him momentarily enchanted by his presence (despite the surprise she has in store for him), and somewhat wryly responds that she wishes to "give light, but… not be light" (that is, unchaste), for she never wants Bassanio to have to worry about her faithfulness.

They embrace and slowly, sensuously start to dance to the cheers of the assembled guests.

But remembering her plan, Portia suddenly breaks away, declaring to herself, "Let God sort all", and standing at arm's length formally proclaims to her new husband, "You are welcome home my Lord!" Bassanio thanks her and bids her greet Antonio, the man to whom he is so personally and closely "bound".

Portia, in thinly veiled jest, agrees that she should be "bound" to him in every way, since she's heard he was rather seriously "bound" for him!

Antonio, adopting an air of modest self-deprecation, dismisses his travails as having been more than compensated for.

In anticipation of her planned agenda vis à vis Bassanio, Portia reiterates her welcome to Antonio but politely cuts short their exchange, indicating that his welcome will be demonstrated most fully by deeds rather than words.

When suddenly "all holy hell breaks loose" with an enraged Nerissa storming into the scene followed in tow by Gratiano protesting she has done him wrong, and that he gave some yet unspecified object to the "judge's clerk", who, as far as his affections are concerned, might as well be castrated, since she's taking his gift so seriously.

Feigning innocence and suppressing amusement, Portia inquires as to the nature of this quarrel so early on in their relationship.

Defensively, Gratiano dismisses the controversy as being over an insignificant "hoop of gold" a "paltry ring" that Nerissa gave him with a kitschy inscription like that of a knife maker, "Love me and leave me not".

Nerissa with feigned outrage pours oil on the fire by demanding of Gratiano how he can disparage the quality of the ring and its poetry when he swore when she gave it to him that he would wear it 'til death and that it would be buried with him in his grave! If not for her, then for the sake of his impassioned promises he should not have parted with it – and he gave it to a "judge's clerk!" By God, that little bastard you gave it to won't live to grow a beard!

Gratiano, at a loss in the face of such vehemence, asserts the possibility that the boy will succeed in growing a beard if he lives long enough to become a man – which in the face of Nerissa's rage may be doubtful.

Nerissa, wryly responds (as yet over Gratiano's head) that, indeed, he'll grow a beard "if a woman live to be a man!".

Gratiano continues his defence (apparently being accused of giving the ring to another woman) that he gave the ring to a "youth", a sort of scrubby little boy no bigger than Nerissa herself (!), a jabbering boy who begged it as payment and he didn't have the heart to deny him.

Portia intervenes, instructing Gratiano that he is, indeed, at fault, to give away his wife's first gift so freely – an object bound to his finger by vows and locked faithfully to his person. She declares that she "gave [her] love a ring and made him swear never to part with it", slyly asserting that Bassanio is standing right here and that she's sure he would never have parted with it for all the world's riches! Portia admonishes Gratiano that he has given his wife more than ample reason to be furious with him and if it were her, she'd be angry too!

Bassanio, observably ashen, says as an aside that he'd better cut off his left hand and claim that he "lost the ring defending it!".

Gratiano, manipulator that he is, tries to deflect attention from his faux pas by snitching on his comrade, revealing that Bassanio gave away his ring too as an act of appreciation to the Judge who begged it of him, and who very much deserved the present. And he was implored by the clerk who wrote the transcript, to part with his ring as well. Neither would accept anything less.

Portia now turns on Bassanio and asks him which ring, exactly, he gave to the Judge? Surely, not the one she gave him, did he?!

Bassanio, caught dead to rights, responds that if he could get away with lying as well as being in error he would deny it, but obviously his finger is bare, the ring is gone.

Portia cuts him to the quick with the accusation that just as his finger is bare of the ring so is his "false heart of truth!". She swears she'll never enter his bed until she sees the ring.

And Nerissa to Gratiano makes the same vow.

Bassanio lovingly implores her, that if she knew to whom he gave the ring, if she knew for whom the ring was given, if she understood why the ring was given, and how reluctantly he gave it away when nothing else would suffice, she would moderate her disapproval.

Portia retorts that if he fully knew the importance of the ring, or half the worth of the woman who gave him the ring, or the responsibility upon him to protect the ring, he would not have parted with it. Who would have been so extreme as to insist on getting such a symbol if he had defended it with any degree of fortitude? Who would have been so immodest as to demand a thing with such solemn value? Portia declares that Nerissa must be right, that she'll bet her life that "some woman had the ring"!

Bassanio, beside himself, swears by his honour and soul that the ring was not given to another woman but rather to a Doctor of

Civil Law who had refused a three thousand ducat payment and begged for the ring instead, which he, initially, denied him causing him to depart in great displeasure, even though he had just saved the life of his dear friend. What was he to do, dear? He felt compelled by guilt and obligation to send the ring after him, rather than be seen as ungrateful and dishonourable. He begs her forgiveness and swears by the stars above that if she'd been there, she, herself, would have demanded the ring from him to give to the honourable attorney.

In response, Portia throws down the gauntlet! She threatens Bassanio not to ever allow that lawyer to approach her house! Since he possesses the gem of her desire which he had sworn to protect, she will become as benevolent as he. She won't deny him anything in her possession, including her own body or her husband's place in bed. She's sure she'll know him (in every sense of the word), so Bassanio had best not be absent from home for one night and he'd better watch her with a hundred eyes like Argus. If he doesn't, if she's left alone, she'll vow to have that Doctor of Laws for her companion.

And Nerissa vows to Gratiano the same intention towards the doctor's clerk! So, he'd better watch out when he leaves her to her own devices.

Gratiano threatens that if she does so, she'd better not let him catch the clerk for if he does, he'll break the young clerk's "pen" (cock)!

Antony interjects, lamenting that these squabbles are about him.

To which Portia reassures him not to be dismayed, that he is welcome nonetheless.

Bassanio pleads with Portia to forgive him the wrong he was forced to commit and that in the presence of the many witnesses gathered there he swears to her by her own beautiful eyes in which he sees himself...

Portia relentlessly cuts him off mocking his vow by picking up on the imagery of him seeing himself in her two eyes, thereby the two of him reflected there representing his "two-faced" self; now that's an oath she'll trust.

Bassanio pleads with her to just forgive this one transgression and by his soul he'll never break another vow to her.

At which point Antonio selflessly intervenes, impressing upon Portia that he had lent his body for Bassanio's benefit, which, had it not been for the gentleman who had his ring would have been sacrificed. That he is prepared to be the assurance again, this time with the forfeiture of his soul, that Bassanio will never again break faith with her, knowingly.

In response to which Portia benevolently hands him the ring, admonishing him to instruct his friend to keep it better than the first time.

Antonio passes the ring to Bassanio instructing him to swear to keep it.

Upon seeing the ring, Bassanio is amazed to discover it is the same one that he gave the Doctor. Portia, however, is not through with him yet, and explains her possession of the doctor's ring by apologising to Bassanio for having slept with him!

And Nerissa follows suit with Gratiano, asking his pardon for having slept with that scrubby "doctor's clerk" the night before in exchange for his ring.

Gratiano, in exasperation claims that they're being cheated on before they deserve it, like fixing the roads in the summer when it's not necessary!

Portia, with calm satisfaction, declares to the aggrieved husbands to calm down – they all look addled.

She takes out a letter which she suggests they read at their leisure. It states, she says, that it comes from Bellario in Padua. It reveals that Portia played the judge Balthasar and Nerissa was the clerk. Lorenzo will attest that she set out for Belmont at the same time they did and only just arrived having not yet entered her house. Turning to Antonio, she once again tells him that he is welcome and that she has a further surprise for him.

She hands Antonio a second letter. Telling him to open the letter she relates that three of his ships have suddenly reached harbour laden with great wealth. And he'll never guess what a strange turn of events brought this letter into her possession.

Antonio declares he is dumbfounded.

Bassanio, emerging from his state of jealousy and shock, asks Portia, incredulously, if she was the Judge without him knowing?

And Gratiano, now catching on with relief, enquires of Nerissa if she were the clerk which will make him a "cuckold?".

To which Nerissa responds, puckishly, yes, but the clerk that never intends to do so unless he grows to be a man!

Bassanio, with romantic abandon, addresses his sweet advocate, who he says will be his "bedfellow", and when he's absent may sleep with his wife!

Antonio, having read the letter in its entirety, tells Portia that she has given him both his life and the means to maintain himself, for the letter confirms that his ships have safely come ashore.

Portia then greets Lorenzo declaring that her "clerk" has some good news for him, as well.

Yes! Nerissa affirms jovially and she'll give it to him without charge!

Handing him a document from the court, Nerissa informs Lorenzo and Jessica that she is giving them a special deed and will from "the rich Jew" leaving them all he owns after his death. Lorenzo, joyously declares that these "fair ladies...drop manna in the way of starvèd people!".

Portia observes it is nearly morning and she's sure there are more questions to be answered regarding these events. She recommends they go into the house where she promises to answer all truthfully and in full.

Gratiano, in peak form, pipes up with the risqué comment that the first thing his Nerissa will have to answer under oath is whether she'd rather wait 'til tomorrow night to go to bed or go to bed immediately with only two hours 'til morning! But when morning comes, he'll wish it were still dark so he might sleep with the advocate's clerk! In any event he'll never worry about anything more in life than "keeping safe Nerissa's ring". (And with that and a swift slap on her derrière, they lustfully exit!)

At this point, the band instinctively strikes up one last number, *J'attendrai*, which Bassanio and Portia lovingly join to dance with the other guests.

Lorenzo motions to Jessica to join him, as well, which she does with her head over his shoulder hiding from his gaze the growing turmoil rising in her face. Finally, her crisis of conscience is too much to hide, and she breaks away in tears towards the house, her exit bringing the gathering to a momentary standstill...

(Blackout).

[5.1a – insert – Forced Conversion]

Darkness. Lights come up on a tableau of the Belmont crowd during their party, followed by the sound of Ave Verum Corpus and the sight of an angelic boys' choir emerging on a riser behind a scrim in the background. A procession enters with two thuggish looking monks (godfathers), faces hidden by hoods, conveying a barely ambulatory Shylock to the ritual font.

The chorus builds to the climax of a single soprano voice, at which point Shylock's head is forcefully pulled backward as he is immersed in the pool by one of the monks, who, throwing back his own head with a maniacal laugh is revealed to be ... Gratiano!

The conversion scene then goes black while the Belmont scene sparks to life quickly dismissing Jessica's "strange" emotional departure with resumed laughter, music, dancing, and chatter, playing off in a frivolous vein the laughter of the monk – punctuating the dichotomy between the two worlds we are witnessing. The lights dim to black as the party continues.

[5.1b – insert]

Lights come up on Shylock as he stumbles into his darkened basement a devastated man. He collapses in a chair centre stage, dimly lit in the surrounding darkness, staring vacantly before him. Suddenly he crumbles, overwhelmed by the magnitude of the abuses and the mania he has suffered. He sobs alone, uncontrollably, surrounded by shadows.

Suddenly, out of the darkness, a strong hand firmly clasps his shoulder as we see the young members of the Irgun (two men and one woman) emerge into the light around him. The young woman kneels by his side and kisses his hand as Shylock stares uncomprehendingly into her eyes as if she were his own Jessica. The group are seen to physically console him speaking sotto voce in his ear out of range of the audience. As their ministrations take effect, we see Shylock slowly strengthen and stiffen his spine, his face hardening with sober resolve now observably different from the wild excesses that brought him to trial with Antonio.

His new comrades urge him to rise. One places a Tanakh before him. The other reveals a pistol which he places on top of the holy book, firmly guiding Shylock's hand to the weapon.

As Shylock confronts the prospect of armed resistance a muted hum of aching and weeping is heard followed by the emerging faces and forms behind a scrim of a growing multitude of refugees of all ages (featuring the little girl of his encounter at the Haifa docks) as if speaking to him directly.

The impact of this ghostly multitude registers in his face as he takes up the gun and commits to armed struggle with an oath repeating his remonstrance to Antonio: "The villainy you teach me, I will execute..."

Blackout. Beat.

Just as the audience think all is over, there issues forth a deafening explosion that shakes the theatre. A huge projection of the shattered east wing of the King David Hotel emerges to dominate the stage, accompanied by a reprise of the Ave Verum Corpus.

In the darkness the unmistakable voice of Golda Meir addressing the 22nd Zionist Congress in Basle, Switzerland in 1946 is heard again, uninterrupted, with her words projected onto a large screen, (UC):

Why are we now pressing our demand for a Jewish state... as a desperate, immediate need? We understood this necessity the moment that we 600,000 Jews in Palestine... stood powerless to rescue hundreds and thousands of Jews, perhaps millions, from certain death. The only obstacle between our readiness to rescue the Jews of Europe and the terrible certainty that death awaited them at Hitler's hands... was a political regulation laid down by strangers – the White Paper! The British government stood between us and millions of Jews lost in Europe...

Song of Songs (Asma Asmaton) *by Mikos Theodorakis, sung by Maria Farantouri, rises, followed slowly by the house lights.*

AFTERWORD
Journey's End for Now

The course I've travelled in pursuit of Shylock has had many turns and byways, reflecting a determined search for an artistic end: an interpretation of *MV* that places Shylock in the realm of the human and discredits a long history of one-dimensional bigotry and stereotype associated with the part. Shylock is a flawed human being to be sure, a vessel seemingly cracked beyond repair. But it must be remembered that he is a human vessel whose condition is the product of some cruelly rough handling – a condition that demands understanding and a penetrating grasp of his circumstances if he is to be truthfully and rightly portrayed.

My journey and the choices made may seem unorthodox and idiosyncratic, but I believe all efforts at original interpretation must be so and, in this instance, I felt a special need to trek off the beaten path. During my travels I've focused on elements that were of special significance to me emotionally and which I felt would lead to my destination. It was never my assumption that my itinerary would necessarily appeal to all travellers. But I did hope that some of the sights and sounds along the way might hold interest for a wider audience irrespective of their desired destinations.

Once again, I must reference a great guide on the actor's road, Sanford Meisner, who told generations of students that an actor's intelligence is not an intellectual intelligence but rather an emotional one. I believe that an actor's preparation must be consistent with that understanding and facilitate an emotional grasp of his character above all else, not simply observe the general colour of the landscape around him or create an assembly of facts without emotional content.

The academic or literary critic has the luxury of "refined indecision" (some call it "balance"), but the actor does not. Actors must conjure up idiosyncratic emotional spirits and display them in a very public way. They cannot hedge their bets dramatically, qualify them to the point of ineffectuality, or shy away from emotionally disturbing thoughts or visions – that way lies death in performance.

Thus, I open myself to the criticism of those preoccupied with the intellect rather than the emotions and disinclined to engage with the often-tortuous paths of the actor's preparation. The greatest achievements in performance are often the least premeditated, predictable, or comfortable and no absolute formula exists for achieving them. How well the results please or move an audience is what the "theatrical gamble" is about at every performance. Thus, actors cannot be intellectually or emotionally neutral, they must make demonstrative choices even at the risk of being wrong.

In short actors must be emotional heroes not cowards.

I have not attempted to address here the wider question of rehearsal techniques, improvisation, vocal exercises, and textual analysis required to bring Shakespeare to life and to free, as the great acting and voice teacher Kristin Linklater has written, 'Shakespeare's voice' embedded in the text.[47] That is a rich and fascinating field in its own right, indispensable to all Shakespeare work but beyond the scope of my efforts here.

I have focused, instead, on a concept and setting for *MV* supported by historical argument and memoir that I feel will provide insight into Shylock's emotional life and behaviour in fully human terms – a goal that I judge to be imperative, morally, and aesthetically. These are elements which I hope will provide a necessary emotional foundation for the work to follow and stimulate further discoveries in rehearsal and performance. For no matter how effectively the natural voice is freed, it must reflect an emotional life of substance in order to be liberated.

The audience is free to accept or reject the results of this process but must never be left unclear about the choices made or be unmoved by them.

There may be those who will find fault with my analysis or consider it "a bridge too far" from a serious discussion of Shakespeare. But if my unorthodoxy, or the vehemence of my critique, or the modern setting I propose, force them to take a second look at *MV* and analyse deeply why they reject my views, a worthwhile purpose may still have been served.

SCENESCAPES

The Trials of Shylock

General Allenby enters Jerusalem, 11th December 1917.

[*Previous page* shows detail from Arthur Szyk, My People. Samson in the Ghetto (The Battle of the Warsaw Ghetto) 1945.].

New York Herald, 11th December 1917.

British soldiers march past David's Citadel, Jerusalem 1917.

Scots Guard Brass Band 1937.

Lord Peel and commission at the Jerusalem War Cemetery, Mount Scopus 1936.

The Jewish Brigade Group. First all Jewish brigade, British army 1944, WW2.

Arthur Szyk, "We Will Never Die"
Memorial Pageant, program cover, Madison Square Garden 1943.

Palmach 'German Squad' Anti-Nazi Partisans in training.
(An elite unit of German speakers formed to counter possible Nazi invasion of Palestine.)

The Jews of Mandatory Palestine vs. the Nazi Mufti (New York Times, May 14 1948).
(*Note: Before the restoration of the modern State of Israel the Zionists were referred to as 'Palestinians'. The Grand Mufti of Jerusalem, Hadj Amin el-Husseini, was a Nazi ally and collaborator.*)

A pioneer views a new settlement, Kibbutz Yehiam, founded by the socialist Zionist Hashomer Hatzair youth movement in the western Upper Galilee.

Members of Kibbutz Kfar Ruppin in Northern Israel work in an area swamp in 1940.
Image by Kluger Zoltan/Israeli Government Press Office.

Nursery children on a Kibbutz in British Mandatory Palestine.

March of United Kibbutz Movement Youth.

Jewish and Arab Workers march together in May Day Parade, Tel Aviv 1947.
Government Press Office (Israel).

Palmach fighters, Israel 1948.

Haganah Ship 'Exodus' carrying illegal refugees to Palestine, Haifa Docks 1947.

Royal Army Medical Corpsman attending to a sick Jewish woman on arrival in Haifa, an illegal immigrant being sent to internment on Cyprus.

Aliyah Bet illegal refugee ship 'Theodore Herzl' intercepted by British authorities, Haifa Port 1947.

The illegal immigrant ship 'Yigur' (right) and the 'Henrietta Sold' (left) in Haifa Bay, August 12 1946.
Photo: David Duncan

Illegal immigrants from the ship 'Yigur' boarded onto the vessel 'Empire Rebel' for transport to detention camps in Cyprus.

A mother and daughter from the 'Yigur' being deported to Cyprus.

Palmach aiding 'Aliyah Bet' illegal immigrant ship 'United Nations' Nahariya beach, 1 January 1948.

Prayers at the Western Wall.

Jewish families expelled from the Old City of Jerusalem, Zion's Gate, June 1948.
Photo: John Phillips

Weapons and ammunition discovered by British forces in Operation Bream sweep, Kibbutz Dorot, Mandatory Palestine 1946

British paratroops guard Jewish suspects rounded up in Haifa during cordon-and-sweep operations 1946.

King David Hotel — British Military and Intelligence Services HQ destroyed by Irgun July 22 1946.

Irgun detainees in the Gil Gil internment camp, Kenya British East Africa 1946.

Newspaper boy, Jerusalem.

Mandate's end: British troops leaving Haifa 1948.

Images for a Sephardic Shylock of Greek Origin

German tanks in Saloniki under the Arch of Galerius 1944.

Waffen-SS invade a Greek village, April 1941.

A young woman weeps during the deportation of the Romaniote Jews of Ioannina, Greece on 25 March 1944. *(Almost all were murdered at the Auschwitz-Birkenau death camp.)*

Salonica Mayor, Yiannis Mpoutaris, commemorates the deportation of Salonika's Jews to the Auschwitz death camp.

NOTES

[1] Support for the Jewish people and Zionism came most vociferously and articulately from sympathetic prominent figures in the British establishment itself, rather than from the Zionist leadership.

The latter, including Jabotinsky, Herbert Samuels, Chaim Weizmann and others were confirmed Anglophiles who clung to the naïve expectation that Britain, as "Mother of Parliaments", and then exemplar of liberal government, was pure and principled in its commitment to the restoration of Jewish self-determination and national independence, i.e. the Zionist cause. Either motivated by a state of denial that their program, so hoped for, and so promising, might die at birth, or fearing that overt confrontation with Britain would exacerbate a situation they were powerless to stop, Zionist leaders were strangely reticent in public regarding the machinations of elements, especially within the Colonial Office, with well-known personal animus towards Jews and the Zionist program of the Lloyd George government. Such was not the case with regard to prominent Christian supporters of high rank within the military who evidently knew in greater detail where the antisemites (and the skeletons) were buried.

A case in point was the testimony of Lt. Col. Henry J. Patterson, D.S.O., a distinguished commander of the British Jewish Legion which saw valiant service at Gallipoli and in the campaign to liberate Palestine from Ottoman rule. Colonial Patterson spent an entire career fighting the ingrained anti-Semitism of his superiors and their discrimination towards his troops – a fight which likely compromised his own advancement in the ranks – and went on to become a prominent Christian advocate for the Zionist cause on the world stage.

In his memoirs he recounts how he saw "the beginning of this policy of knifing the Jewish National Home while... commanding the Jewish Legion in Palestine during and after the World War..." It began with the appointment of Lieutenant-General Louis Bols as governor of Palestine, a man Colonel Patterson describes as "the most rabid anti-Semite I had ever met." When he first heard of plans to appoint Bols, he viewed the prospect as a "catastrophe" for the Zionist program and was moved to seek out the prominent Zionist leader, Chaim Weizmann, to warn him of the danger. Patterson told him: "If Bols is appointed Governor of Palestine, he will get every anti-Semite in the Colonial service that he can lay his hands on... and fill the administration with them... If you give him this much of a start, you will never see your National Home." Weizmann, apparently gulled by Bols in a two-hour meeting with him, dismissed his concerns informing Patterson that he had found General Bols "a most charming gentleman" – an assessment he would later come to grievously regret. Bols was appointed and proceeded to do just that. Moreover, according to Patterson, not only did these developments affect the disposition of British administration for many years to come, but "soon infected certain Arab politicians..."

Lieutenant-General Louis Bols, Governor of Palestine

As a result, an attack on Zionism by proxy was initiated, which, under the leadership of Haj Amin el-Husseini, appointed by Britain as the Grand Mufti of Jerusalem (and a future Nazi collaborator), encouraged murderous extremism throughout the territory of the Mandate which savaged not only the Jewish communities of Palestine, but the moderate, law abiding Arab populations amenable to living peacefully with the Jews, as well.

Thus, a passive-aggressive policy of a most murderous kind was initiated, not initially by the Arabs, but by a certain class of reactionary British colonial administrators and military personnel of bigoted inclination intent on subverting the liberal, pro-Zionist policies of the duly elected Liberal government of Great Britain.

(See: Lt. Col. Henry J. Patterson, D.S.O., *Excerpts from Articles and Speeches of the 1930s*, Appendix F, p.542; cited in *Years of Wrath Days of Glory* by Yitshaq Ben-Ami, Robert Speller & Sons, New York, 1982).

[2] Harold Bloom, *Shakespeare: The Invention of the Human* (New York,1998), p.171.

[3] Robert Brustein, interview with Alicia Anstead, *Harvard Arts Blog*, January 25th, 2011

[4] Robert S. Wistrich, Medieval England: A Leader in Antisemitism, (interview: *Jerusalem Center for Public Affairs*, June 11, 2008)

[5] French critic, Pierre Priet, quoted in *Shylock* by John Gross, pp.344-6.
[6] https://www.nytimes.com/1993/04/04/theater/theater-shylock-andnazi-propaganda.html.
[7] John Gross, *Shylock: A Legend and its Legacy* (New York 1992), pp.45-6.
[8] A more sensitive response is detailed in a recollection on p.50.
[9] See video: htttps://www.youtube.com/watch?v=8dLa2WmwOK0.
[10] John Gross, Op. Cit. 7, p.340.
[11] Ibid.
[12] I became aware after having developed a good deal of my conception that an effort at a Palestine setting had been proposed by Charles Marowitz in 1977 in his *Variations on the Merchant of Venice*, a work I have deliberately refrained from reading lest it bleed into my own thinking on the subject. According to a brief description of the Marowitz piece in John Gross's, *Shylock*, Mr. Marowitz created a composite work incorporating elements of *MV* and Marlowe's, *The Jew of Malta*, which is precisely what I would not want to do; my approach being that of rendering Shakespeare's text unaltered in a manner conducive to the interpretation I desire.
[13] Op. Cit. 5
[14] Robert Brustein, *The Tainted Muse*, Yale University Press, New Haven and London, pp.1 and 243.
[15] Keats, John (1899). *The Complete Poetical Works and Letters of John Keats*, Cambridge Edition. Houghton, Mifflin and Company. p.277. (Cited in the article, "Negative Capability", Wikipedia).
[16] In the manner of "The Dramaturg's Speech" from *Buying Brass* by Bertolt Brecht.
[17] 'The hour of the wolf is the hour between night and dawn. It is the hour when most people die, when sleep is the deepest, when nightmares feel most real. It is the hour when the demons are most powerful. The hour of the wolf is also the hour when most children are born.'
[18] Op. Cit. 10
[19] Ibid.
[20] Op. Cit. 6
[21] Wikipedia, Schwartbard Trials.
[22] Op. Cit. 6
[23] The 2001 production at the Royal National Theatre, starring Henry Goodman, directed by Trevor Nunn; and the 2004 film starring Al Pacino, directed by Michael Radford.
[24] Rev. Dr. Walter Wink, *Homosexuality and the Bible*: "And the repugnance felt toward homosexuality was not just that it was deemed unnatural but also that it was considered un-Jewish, representing yet one more incursion of pagan civilization into Jewish life."
[25] For a further discussion of the problem of reconciling the polytheistic implications of Christian belief with its professed monotheism, see: Michael C. Rea, Polytheism and Christian Belief, *Journal of Theological*

Studies, NS, Vol. 57, Pt 1, April 2006.
[26] Aaron Spencer Fogleman, "Jesus is Female: Moravians and Radical Religion in Early America", (Philadelphia, 2007), p. 83.
[27] Richard Kaye, *The Gay & Lesbian Literary Heritage*, ed. Claude J. Summers (New York: Henry Holt,1995.
[28] Ibid.
[29] See James Shapiro, *Shakespeare and the Jews*, (New York 1996), pp.126-30.
[30] Ibid. pp.121-26.
[31] Ibid. p.127.
[32] Ibid. pp.102
[33] Ibid.
[34] Ibid.p113.
[35] See: "Christopher Hitchens and Rabbi Shmuley Boteach Debate on God", (https://www.youtube.com/watch?v=vnMYL8sF7bQ: 36:01).
[36] Flannery, Edward H., *The Anguish of the Jews,* (New York, 1965), p.xi.
[37] James Shapiro, Op. Cit. 27, pp.36-39.
[38] Ibid., pp.93-95, 105.
[39] Ibid. p. 37.
[40] William Shakespeare, *Henry IV, Part One*, (3:2).
[41] Miller, Arthur, *Death of a Salesman*, Act 1
[42] Patrick Stewart, much to his credit, achieved precisely this effect in the excerpt mentioned above.
[43] Bernt Engelmann, *Germany Without Jews*, (New York, October 1984).
[44] John Gross, Op. Cit. 7, p.36.
[45] According to Uri Avneri, long a prominent leftwing Israeli journalist – formerly an early member of the Irgun – Begin was a member of Hashomer Hatzair before it adopted a pro-Soviet line, but the movement was always left-wing and secular, incorporating an amalgam of then "progressive" ideological influences – ranging from socialism to psychoanalysis – from its beginnings. (See: Uri Avneri, Menachem Begin: The Reality, (*WORLDVIEW*, June 1978).
[46] In conversation with leftwing Knesset Member, Meir Pa'il, early 1970s.
[47] Menachem Begin's parents and brother died in Nazi concentration camps (see: Menachem Begin, *Encyclopedia Britannica*; (https://www.britannica.com/biography/Menachem-Begin).
[48] See: *All That Is Interesting* website; The 8 Most Painful Torture Devices of the Middle Ages, June 30, 2016 (http://all-that-isinteresting.com/medieval-torture-devices/2).
[49] see, *Freeing Shakespeare's Voice* by Kristin Linklater.

BIBLIOGRAPHY

Barnavi, Eli, and Eliav-Feldon, Miriam, eds. *A Historical Atlas of the Jewish People.* New York: Schocken Books, 1992.

Ben-Ami, Yitshaq. *Years of Wrath Days of Glory: Memoirs from the Irgun.* New York: Robert Speller and Sons, Publisher, 1982.

Bloom, Harold, ed. *Modern Critical Interpretations: William Shakespeare's The Merchant of Venice.* New York, New Haven, Philadelphia: Chelsea House Publishers, 1986.

Bowyer Bell, J. *Terror out of Zion.* New York: St. Martin's Press, 1977.

Brustein, Robert. *The Tainted Muse: Prejudice and Presumption in Shakespeare and his Time.* New Haven, London: Yale University Press, 2009.

Carrol, James. Constantine's Sword: *The Church and the Jews: A History.* Houghton Mifflin Company, 2001.

Dorril, Stephen. *MI6.* New York: Touchstone (Simon and Schuster), 2000.

Flannery, Edward H. T*he Anguish of the Jews.* New York: The MacMillan Company, 1965.

Gross, John. *Shylock.* New York, London, Toronto, Sydney, Tokyo, Singapore: Simon & Schuster, 1992.

Haber, Eitan. *Menahem Begin: The Legend and The Man.* New York: Delacorte Press, 1978.

Hoffman, Bruce. *Anonymous Soldiers: The Struggle for Israel, 1917-1947.* New York: Alfred A. Knopf, 2015.

Isaac, Rael Jean. I*srael Divided: Ideological Politics in the Jewish State.* Baltimore: The Johns Hopkins University Press, 1977.

Julius, Anthony. *Trials of the Diaspora: A History of Antisemitism in England.* New York: Oxford University Press, 2010.

Kertzer, David I. *The Popes Against the Jews: The Vatican's Role in the Rise of Modern Anti-Semitism.* New York: Knopf, 2001.

Meir, Golda. *A Land of Our Own: An Oral Autobiography.* Edited by Marie Syrkin. New York: G. P. Putnam's Sons, 1973.

Parkes, James. *The Jew in the Medieval Community.* New York: Hermon Press, 1976.

Ranke-Heinemenne, Uta. *Eunuchs for the Kingdom of Heaven: Women Sexuality and the Catholic Church.* New York: Doubleday, 1990.

Segev, Tom. *One Palestine Complete: Jews and Arabs Under the British Mandate*. New York: Henry Holt and Co., LLC

Shapiro, James. *Shakespeare and the Jews.* New York: Columbia University Press, 1996.

Shapiro, James; Greenblatt, Stephen. Correspondence, *New York Review of Books*, October 14, 2010.

Sherman, A.J. *Mandate Days: British Lives in Palestine, 1918-1948.* Baltimore: Johns Hopkins University Press, 2001.

Sternhell, Zeev. *The Founding Myths of Israel.* Princeton, New Jersey: Princeton University Press, 1998.

Wisse, Ruth R. *Jews and Power.* New York: Schocken Books, 2007.

Wistrich, Robert S. *Antisemitism.* New York: Pantheon Books, 1991.

Wyman, David S. *The Abandonment of the Jews: America and the Holocaust 1941-1945*. New York: Pantheon Books, 1985.

INDEX

92nd Street Y	56

A

Actor	1-3, 10, 19, 21, 27-34, 40, 50, 53, 65-70, 76, 83, 188
Adler, Stella	83
Aesthetic	27, 30, 62-3, 88, 189
African American	31, 45, 61, 67, 155
Allegory	33, 35, 110
Anachronism	43-5
ANC African National Congress	28, 80
Antichrist, the	62
Antihero	26, 63-4
Antisemitism	2-5, 9-10, 12-16, 18, 21-9, 33, 35, 40, 42-6, 52, 54-5, 57, 65, 70, 88, 92, 99, 109, 141, 148, 158, 191
Antonio	2, 5, 17, 19, 36, 40-41, 45-50, 53, 60, 67, 77, 91, 93
ARF Armenian Revolutionary Federation	38
Armenia	37-8, 43, 102
Art	29, 35-6
Attitudes	3, 17, 43, 45, 54, 118
Audience	2-3, 10, 16-7, 23-4, 34, 41, 44-5, 53, 56, 80, 88, 97, 107, 116-8, 184-5, 187-9
Avarice	17, 46, 151

B

Balfour, Arthur	6
Balthazar	49
Banks	17, 60, 101 *see also moneylender*
Barton, John Sir	12
Bassanio	17, 26, 41, 47-8
Begin, Menachem	79-81, 83, 214
Bellario	49
Belmont	22-3, 49, 51-2, 62, 77, 92

Ben-Gurion, David	78
Bergman, Ingmar	29
Berlin	38
Bevan, Aneurin	6
Bevin, Ernrst	16
Bible	11, 64, 113
Biblical	see Bible
Bigotry	4, 15-6, 21-5, 57, 62, 87, 94, 187
Bloom, Harold	9
Bloomsbury	51-2, 104, 115
Bond (Shylock's)	54
Brecht, Bertolt	27
Britain	4, 6, 14, 51-2, 56, 72, 79, 81, 88, 91, 191
British Mandatory Palestine	4-5, 23, 78, 82, 88, 91, 93, 97, 107
Brustein, Robert	9
Brutus, Marcus Junius	38, 102
Business	13-4, 16-8, 41, 46, 50, 60, 67-8, 81, 89

C

Caesar, Julius	38
Canard	2, 4, 55, 58-60
Cannibalism	55-6, 80
Capitalism	17
Caricature	18, 42, 63
Carnovsky, Morris	66
Castration	54-5
Chaucer, Geoffrey	16
Cherry Orchard, The	66
Christ	see Jesus Christ
Christian	3, 5-6, 11-7, 19, 22-3, 25, 32-3, 35-7, 40-3, 45-62, 66, 76-7, 80-1, 90-2
Christian Zionists	6
Church	17, 48, 57-8, 69-70
Churchill, Winston	6
Circumcision	52-56
Class System	4, 6, 14-6, 22, 46-7, 512, 65, 70-2, 88, 91
Cobbett, William	16
Comedy	3, 9, 33
Contradiction	10, 23, 36, 42-3, 46, 69, 74
Conversion	3, 81, 90, 92, 183
Coward, Noel	72
Crime	4, 17, 23, 37, 68, 87
Crossman, Richard	6

Czar   57

D

Death of a Salesman   *63*
Deicide   41
Derision   3, 13, 16, 25, 33, 44, 55-6, 69
Desdemona   *see Othello*
Devil, the   15, 18
Diamond   12, 68
Diaspora   15, 78
Dickens, Charles   6
Director   2, 9-10, 21, 48, 53-5, 65
Disraeli, Benjamin   15
Drury Lane   20

E

East, the   14-5, 88
Eliot, T.S.   45
Elite   3, 5, 37
Elizabethan   6, 11, 44-5, 53, 70, 92
Enlightenment   11, 44-5, 62
Everyman   63
Existentialism   4, 16, 47-8, 64, 80, 91
Exploitation   15, 23, 56, 89

F

Fairy Tale   22, 51
Fantasy   22, 29, 33, 35, 46, 51, 62, 94
Finance   *see business*
Fiorentino, Ser Giovanni   43-4
Foot, Michael   6
Foreign(er)   44, 49, 56, 75-7, 87
French Foreign Legion   39
Freud, Sigmund   54

G

General Strike 1926   70-1
Genocide   4, 37-8
Germany   14, 35, 76, 97
Ghetto   76, 81
Gladstone, W.E.   15-6
God   21-2, 37-8, 48, 53, 60

283

Gratiano	91
Greenblatt, Stephen	18-9
Grief	68-9, 89, 92, 113, 117, 137, 142
Gross, John	11, 22, 35-6, 76
Group Theatre, The	66
Guignol (Grand)	11, 42

H

Haganah	6, 81, 91, 174
Halacha	41, 46
Hamas	57, 191
Hamlet	29-30, 38
Hashomer, Hatzair	79
Heart, the	31, 40, 54
Hecht, Ben	83
Herzl, Theodore	75
Hitchens, Christopher	56
Hollywood	60, 73, 83
Holocaust	4, 24, 26, 35, 55, 57, 82, 91
Homeland	91
Homicide	40 *see also murder*
Homosexuality	47-9, 165
Houseman, John & Smith, Barney	16
Hypocrisy	22, 24, 36, 42, 49, 51, 81

I

Iago	*see Othello*
Ideology	15, 78-81, 89
Il Pecorone	*43*
Imperialism	4, 51, 67, 79, 81, 88, 92
Intention	3, 9, 10, 22, 25-7, 33, 35, 43, 45
IRA	28, 80
Irgun Zvai Leumi	79, 81-3, 91, 93
Irony	35-7, 41, 76
Israel	3, 22-3, 54, 70, 78, 80, 100, 191
Israel, Rabbi Mennaseh Ben	55

J

Jabotinsky, Ze'ev	79
Jealousy	14
Jefferson, Thomas	36

Jessica	89
Jesus Christ	22, 58-9, 62, 69
Jew of Malta, The	*18, 44*
Jewish Agency for Palestine	79, 91
Jewish Legion	6
'Jim Crow'	67
John Neumeier	89, 113
Judaism	11, 48, 56, 60, 70
Julius, Anthony	15-16
Justice	3, 5, 30, 37-9, 46, 61-2, 64, 82-3, 92

K

Keats, John	26
Kermode, Frank	22
Kibbutz Beit Zera	70
Knesset	80

L

La Dame Aux Camélias	*89, 113*
Labour Party (UK)	6, 78, 80
Labour Zionist	79-80
LAMDA	68
Launcelot Gobbo	91
Law	13, 22, 37, 39, 41, 46, 75, 92
Leah	88-9
Levantine	76, 81
Linklater, Kristin	1, 31-2, 188
Lloyd George, David	6
Loman, Willy/Linda	63
London	3, 14, 37, 68
Long Wharf Theatre	66
Love	11, 22, 33, 45, 47-8

M

Manchester Circle	6
Marlowe, Christopher	18
Martyr	21, 23, 62-3, 88
Marxism	15
Matalon, Vivian	65
Materialism	22, 46-7
Media	60
Medieval	4, 18, 46, 54-60

285

Meisner, Sandford	31-4, 66, 188
Melancholy	17, 47
Mercy	22, 50-1, 73, 82
Miller, Arthur	63
Mizrahi	74
"Money-grubber"	16-17
Moneylender	14, 16-8, 22, 33-4, 43, 49, 62, 67
Monty Python	46
Morality	36
Mosley, Oswald	93
Murder	12-5, 31, 37-9, 41, 55, 57-60, 68, 80, 83
Muslim	53
Mutilation	2, 41, 44, 53, 80

N

Nationalism	16, 24, 39, 67, 75-80, 82, 88
Nazi	4, 10, 31, 35, 45, 75-6, 83, 88-9, 93, 97
Negative Capability	26
New Testament	48
Norms	42, 47, 52, 89, 92

O

Old Testament	47-8, 54, 56
Olivier, Laurence	77, 158
Oppression	9, 24, 27, 83, 87, 94, 111
Orthodoxy	28, 57
Orwell, George	16
Othello	14, 52-3
Ottoman Empire	38

P

Palestine	4-6, 23, 52, 78-82, 88, 90-3
Palmach	81, 91
Paradigm	23
Paris	39-40
Pasha, Talaat	37-8
Patterson, Henry J.	6
Perception	3, 25-6, 32, 37, 89
Petliura, Symon	39
Poland	79
Ponentine	76
Portia	19, 36, 48-51, 73-4, 77, 91-2
"Pound of flesh"	13, 40, 42, 48, 55, 60, 80, 91

Prejudice	4-5, 11, 14-7, 22-5, 34-5, 44, 53-4, 57-8, 62, 76, 88, 90-2, 118
Prima Facie	35-6
Producer	2, 10, 18, 31, 35, 47, 53, 74, 77
Prospero	29-30
Protestant	46
Protocol	33
Psychoanalysis	54-5

R

Racism	18, 24, 45, 50, 61, 75-6
Rage	2, 4, 31, 48, 88, 91-2
Reformation	46
Reik, Theodore	54
Renaissance	57
Revolution	28, 38-9, 67, 80, 82, 91, 94
Rialto	22, 41, 51
Rights of Man	36
Roman	48, 76-7
Romanticism	21, 26, 88
Rorschach	29
Roth, Philip	191
Rothschild	72
RSC	12
Russell, Bertrand	16
Russia	28, 39
Russian Orthodox	57

S

Saint Paul	54, 58
Schwartzbard, Sholem	39-40
Secularism	11, 54
Setting	3, 5, 22-3, 52, 76, 78, 81-2, 87-92, 189
Sex	47-8, 52-3, 58
Shakespeare, William	1-6, 10-12, 16, 19, 21, 24-9, 32-3, 35, 37-8, 42, 45, 53, 60-1, 63, 66, 73, 76-7, 80, 88, 188-9
Shapiro, James	19
Shaw, George Bernard	12
Socialist-Zionism	*see Labour-Zionist*
Society	5, 12-17, 25, 35, 43-5, 51, 53, 57-8, 60, 76-7, 89-92
Staging	10, 24
Stanislavsky	12, 66
Stereotypes	2, 4, 16-8, 22, 25, 57, 60-2, 65, 81, 88, 94, 187

Stern Group	79, 91
Stewart, Patrick	12
Suchet, David	12
Symbols	13, 22, 26, 48, 53-5, 62, 67, 71
Sympathy	2, 5, 21, 27-8, 38, 43-44, 50-51, 55, 67-8, 71, 79, 83

T

Tehlirian, Soghomon	37-9
Ten Commandments	37
The Group Theatre	66
Theatre	1, 17, 33, 66, 74
Torres, Henri	39
Trade	*see business*
Tradition	3-4, 10-14, 18-19, 22, 25, 35, 37, 42, 46-7, 51, 58, 62, 78, 81, 88, 94
Trauma	4, 26, 90
Treatment	3-5, 87, 90
Trial Scene	49, 53, 73, 77, 157-166
Tropes	56
Truth	22, 24, 27, 33, 44, 51, 62, 64, 67, 79, 187
Tubal	88

U

Ukraine	39
Usury	*see moneylender*

V

Vengeance	12, 21-2, 92
Venice	2-3, 13-4, 23, 37, 48, 51, 68, 76-7, 88, 91

W

Wall St	60
WASP	68
West, the	11, 23, 25, 34, 46, 58-9, 62, 76, 87
White Russian	39
Wilson, Harold	6
Wingate, Orde	6
Wistrich, Robert	1
WWI	6, 38, 97
WWII	9, 79, 97

X,Y,Z

Xenophobia	44, 76
Yishuv, the	79, 89, 93
Young Guard, the	79
Zionism	6, 70, 75, 78-80
Zionist Revisionism	78-9

ABOUT THE AUTHOR

With a resume that includes notable acting roles as well as university-level teaching, this is Alan Bergreen's first book on Shakespeare; long in the making. He taught Acting, Voice Production, and Speech at the *University of Southern California, School of Dramatic Arts*, as well as Speech for Foreign Students at the *USC Marshall School of Business*. He trained as an actor and teacher with Sanford Meisner in his private studios in New York and Hollywood and completed the *Voice and Shakespeare* course with Kristin Linklater, receiving the postgraduate diploma in Acting from the *London Academy of Music & Dramatic Art (LAMDA)*, and pursuing scene study with Vivian Matalon and through Lynn Redgrave's *Shakespeare Master Class*.

"*I am keenly interested in the training process and the importance of the theatre as a social force for good and an agent of community. My perspectives on theatre have been shaped by a diversity of international influences, including: French director, Guy Romans, former head of the Vieux Colombier Theatre School of Paris and heir to the theatre of Jacques Copeau, Louis Jouvet and Charles Dullin; Russian family background closely associated with the Yiddish Art Theatre in the U.S. and former Soviet Union, and exposure to the theatres of Israel (Habima, Cameri, Haifa Theatre, etc.).*"

He has also worked with directors of the *Royal Shakespeare Company, Royal Court Theatre, The Old Vic* and the *Welsh National Theatre,* appearing in the *Royal National Theatre* production of *An Enemy of the People*, starring Ian McKellen at the *Ahmanson Theatre* in Los Angeles.

Extending beyond the arts, his experience spans investigations and Mid-East affairs in the U.S. Congress, extensive political engagement and volunteer service, writing and political commentary.

www.ingramcontent.com/pod-product-compliance
Lightning Source LLC
Chambersburg PA
CBHW041304110526
44590CB00028B/4242